COLLECTOR'S
COMPASS™

Jewelry

   Bothell, Washington

Credits

President . . . . .Nancy J. Martin
CEO . . . . Daniel J. Martin
Publisher . . . . .Jane Hamada
Editorial Director . . . . Mary V. Green
Editorial Project Manager. . . . . .Tina Cook
Series Editor . . . . Christopher J. Kuppig
Design and Production Manager . . . . Stan Green
Design . . . . Bonnie Mather
Series Concept . . . . Michael O. Campbell

Collector's Compass™: Jewelry
© 2000 by Martingale & Company

Martingale & Company
PO Box 118
Bothell, WA 98041-0118 USA
www.martingale-pub.com

Printed in Canada
05 04 03 02 01 00   6 5 4 3 2 1

Library of Congress Cataloging-in-Publication Data
Collector's Compass: Jewelry
  p. cm. — (Collector's compass)
  ISBN 1-56477-345-0
  1. Barbie dolls—Collectors and collecting. I. Series

NK7304.J48 2000
739.27'075—dc21   00-042368

Mission Statement
We are dedicated to providing quality products and service by working together to inspire creativity and to enrich the lives we touch.

CONTENTS

Unsigned fan brooch

FOREWORD

As America's favorite hobby, collecting is exciting, gratifying, and above all, fun—but without the right knowledge, you could be destined for disappointment. Luckily, you've just found the most resourceful and inspiring series of guidebooks available to help you learn more about collecting. The Collector's Compass series approaches collecting in a whole new way, making it easy to learn about your favorite collectible categories—from the basics to the best-kept secrets.

The International Society of Appraisers (ISA) is pleased to be associated with the Collector's Compass series. As the ISA celebrates twenty years of professional education and certification of personal property appraisers, who currently specialize in over two hundred areas of expertise, we remain committed to setting the highest standards for our accredited members. The Collector's Compass series of reference books reflects the ISA's dedication to quality and integrity.

Christian Coleman, ISA CAPP, Ret.
Executive Director, International Society of Appraisers

*I*NTRODUCTION

Whether it means setting the alarm clock for Saturday morning yard sales, watching "Antiques Roadshow," or chasing down childhood memories on eBay, collecting has become America's favorite hobby. The joy of finding treasure amid the clutter of a tag sale or a screen full of online offerings is infectious. Who could resist a pastime that combines the fun of shopping, the thrill of the hunt, the lure of a bargain, and the pride of ownership?

Throngs of novice collectors are joining experienced veterans in online bidding and weekend "antiquing" expeditions. If you count yourself among them, this book is for you.

The editors of Collector's Compass realized that today's collectors needed more information than what was available, in an accessible and convenient format. Going beyond available price and identification guides, Collector's Compass books introduce the history behind a particular collectible, the fascinating aspects that make it special, and exclusive tips on where and how to search for exciting pieces.

Furthermore, the Collector's Compass series is uniquely reliable. Each volume is created by a carefully chosen team of dealers, appraisers, and other experts. Their collaboration ensures that each title will contain accurate and current information, as well as the secrets they've learned in a lifetime of collecting.

We hope that in the Collector's Compass series we have addressed every area essential to building a collection. Whether you're a newcomer or an experienced collector, we're sure this series will lead you to new treasures. Enjoy the adventure!

JEWELRY AS A COLLECTIBLE

Collecting jewelry is an age-old hobby that has enjoyed sharply escalating popularity during the past decade. Admirers are attracted because each piece is an individual work of art, and jewelry affords an opportunity for display that few collectibles can claim: instead of being cataloged, stored, and periodically dusted, it can be worn and enjoyed daily. Indeed, for some it is as necessary as clothing; for others, a comforting companion—remember "Diamonds are a girl's best friend"?

Perhaps your interest in jewelry is newfound, or you've long admired a friend's collection and think you might enjoy having one of your own. Or maybe you are already committed to expanding a cherished collection of Victorian brooches inherited from your great-grandmother. Whatever the case, this book will help you explore ways to build a collection—by designer, materials, theme, motif, era, or manufacturer. Then it will guide you through the marketplace in a way that helps you have fun during your quest while you gain the knowledge you'll need to avoid common errors.

Silver Scottish pebble brooch, c. 1870

Late-nineteenth to early twentieth-century mosaic brooch

Popular in the Victorian era, mourning jewelry frequently included the hair of a lost loved one, as in this hairwork cravat pin.

The Special Allure of Jewelry

Far more than other collectibles, jewelry speaks volumes about the collector. A woman who sports colorful Bakelite bracelets, pins, and necklaces is telling the world that she is upbeat and madcap, attracted to bright colors and fun concepts. A man who wears a somber piece of Victorian mourning jewelry on his lapel conveys his connection to history and signals that he is a sentimental, introspective person. Among fashion accessories, jewelry reveals more about the taste and sophistication of its wearer than shoes, a scarf, or a belt.

Antique and collectible jewelry has devotees for other reasons. An almost limitless variety is available, making it suitable for every taste and pocketbook. Most of it is relatively sturdy and can survive handling and wear. And reasonably priced collectible jewelry from times past often exhibits craftsmanship of a caliber that is typically only available to the extremely well-heeled.

Some collectors have an affinity for a particular era because of the prevailing style of the time: jewelry often exemplifies that aesthetic, thus making it a standout for these collectors. For example, cameos—those skillfully carved portraits achieved by cutting away layers of shell, hardstone, lava, or gemstone—have always reflected the predominant concept of beauty. Thus, Victorian-era cameos depict long, straight, aquiline "Roman" noses because that was the ideal. Cameos of the 1920s have smaller, upturned noses, reflecting a more contemporary ideal of beauty. It is also possible to date portrait cameos based upon hairstyles, dress, and accessories.

Collections are, for some, a status symbol—a way of announcing monetary success by wearing obviously expensive jewels. A closely related motive is pride of ownership.

For a fortunate few, a hobby that begins with the sheer love of ornaments becomes a business, a way to make a living. Still others collect to recapture the past or to hold on to a special memory. For instance, numerous collectors specialize in baby jewelry. One woman collects wide-band, yellow-gold baby rings, beautifully embellished, but without stones. She wears the rings strung on a gold chain around her neck.

Often, people who don't set out to collect jewelry wind up doing so as a result of other passions. Aficionados of vintage fashion collect period jewelry, as do collectors of boudoir items, such as vanity jars and fans. Handbag and shoe collectors dabble in jewelry. Many Art Deco furniture and decorative accessories collectors also collect Art Deco jewelry. And collectors of all categories of World War II artifacts seek out examples of sweetheart jewelry, sent home by soldiers to their loved ones during the war.

Finding Collectible Jewelry

Jewelry is a tempting field for collectors because of its great presence in the market; in fact, it is ubiquitous. You'll find jewelry spread across tables at every flea market, lined up in individual boxes at every antiques shop, and glittering in showcases at high-end shows. At either extreme, some of the jewelry is lovely, exquisitely designed, and constructed of fine materials; some of it is just junk. Most of it falls somewhere in between. Your primary challenge is to separate the wheat from the chaff.

As you may have observed, prices can range from pocket change to many thousands of dollars. This variety and abundance can be daunting. It becomes easier to shop once you've selected an area of interest; on the other hand, you shouldn't narrow your focus too soon. It's a good idea to sample several venues; become familiar with the variety available and asking prices before deciding on a specialty.

Read trade papers, such as *Antique Trader,* especially the classified ads; they will provide a good overview of collecting trends and keep you apprised of availability and price ranges. (See "Essential Background for Jewelry Collectors" for complete subscription information.)

In "Before You Start Collecting," we'll delve into each venue in more detail and provide the tools to help you collect confidently and wisely wherever you shop—but just to give you an idea of the possibilities, here's a quick tour of the marketplace.

Gold heart locket, c. 1900

Garage, Rummage, and Tag Sales

As recently as ten years ago, you could easily find high-quality costume jewelry—pieces that may contain precious metals but not precious gemstones—at garage sales, flea markets, and church rummage sales. Most people considered anything not made of gold to be junk. Today, costume jewelry is in great demand, and it's a lot more difficult to locate high-end pieces and buy them for a song. However, if you do your homework and you know what you're looking for, you can still find real bargains.

A word of caution from one expert: sellers at yard and garage sales often price a piece too high because they've never seen another one like it and incorrectly assume it is rare.

Estate Sales and Auctions

Mourning pendant with hair in Prince of Wales curls

Wonderful finds can be made at estate sales and auctions if you are persistent and willing to spend the time hunting and sorting. You will run into stiff competition from dealers and other collectors, so beware: the temptation to forget your budget in the heat of bidding can be overwhelming.

If there is an auction catalog, study it beforehand so you can bid with confidence, having consulted whatever references you may have to authenticate a piece and judge its rarity, condition, and value. Never assume that the auction house or estate seller has tested jewelry for metal content or genuine stones unless documentation is provided.

As your collection matures and you begin to seek specific items, specialized auctions may prove to be the best places to find pieces you "must" have.

Organized Flea Markets

While jewelry is likely to be plentiful, shopping at flea markets is a hit-or-miss way to find things. It is definitely worth your while to visit a few flea markets to become familiar with what's available. Always tell dealers what you're looking for; they're likely to know their inventories well enough to pinpoint pieces that you may have missed.

Specialized Dealers

The most efficient way to find the jewelry you want at good prices is to develop a relationship with a reliable supplier. Seek out a dealer who specializes in what you collect and tell her what you want to buy. It takes time and effort to cultivate such a relationship, but if you become a steady customer, it's possible that she'll become an extra set of eyes and ears for you in the marketplace.

One expert collector of period jewelry advises that it's best to buy only through specialized dealers who have a permanent place of business, guarantee the authenticity of merchandise, offer jewelry-related services as well as a large selection, and provide detailed receipts.

Antiques and Collectibles Shows

Shows can be great fun and usually offer interesting merchandise. The more specialized the show, the more likely you are to add to your collection—but that's not the only reason to go.

Jewelry on display at an antiques show

> ### *Treasure in Unlikely Places*
>
> A dealer and respected authority on antique jewelry arrived at an estate sale to find the jewelry cases surrounded by a mass of people. She decided to look around the rest of the house until the crowd subsided.
>
> In an upstairs bedroom, taped to a nightstand, she found a chain marked $1. It looked like a garden-variety pull-chain for a light fixture, but on close examination the dealer noticed that there was a fine design on each tiny bead and link, as well as a broken portion of a clasp at one end. She forked over a dollar bill and, to her delight, now owned a 32-inch platinum necklace!

Typical ad from a trade paper

Shows provide terrific opportunities to find out what's going on and to meet both dealers and collectors of jewelry and allied categories. Obviously, some collectors will be in direct competition with you and won't wish to share the time of day, but you will meet others who can't wait to show off the expertise gleaned through their years of collecting. As you develop relationships, some of these people will watch out for your "wants" in their travels, especially if you reciprocate.

Web Sites and Internet Auctions

There are many Web sites that deal exclusively in jewelry. Many offer historical and educational material on topics, from repairing your own jewelry to dating it by the trademarks. A number of sites will be recommended under specific subjects in this book.

Search through Internet auctions, especially the archives of auctions recently completed, to see what prices your favorite types of jewelry are realizing. Always check "seller's other auctions" when you find something you like—there may be more.

Associations and Newsletters

You may want to join three important groups. Membership can help educate you and introduce you to other enthusiasts—who often prove to be great sources of jewelry!

The collector's association called **Vintage, Fashion and Costume Jewelry** publishes a quarterly newspaper full of educational articles. Members advertise items for sale. The group also has a biannual convention in Providence, Rhode Island, the historical center of American costume jewelry.

Jewelcollect is an online group with an e-mail mailing list server, a bulletin board, and an online jewelry auction, all free.

The American Society of Jewelry Historians publishes a newsletter with upcoming events around the world, news of members, articles on interesting topics, reviews of jewelry books, and discounts. In the past, it has offered free passes to the International Jewelers Association Las Vegas Antique Jewelry Show.

Eventually, you will want to join one or more clubs whose members and literature are geared specifically to your collecting specialty. There's at least one group for those who collect in every imaginable category.

See "Essential Background for Jewelry Collectors" for more details and contact information on these organizations, along with a listing of Web-site addresses.

Organizing Your Collection

There are almost as many ways to collect as there are collectors. Some popular organizing principles are discussed here, but you may discover that coming up with your own collecting scheme is as much fun as buying a special treasure. You may also find that your collecting interests grow and change as you become more knowledgeable.

Artist or Designer

Jewelry certainly lends itself to being collected by designer. Some collectors concentrate on the work of a single artist, acquiring examples of his work from the beginning to the end of his career, the way one collects the work of a particular painter.

Lovely collections have been built solely of the works of a single designer, such as Kenneth J. Lane, Alfred Phillipe, McClelland Barclay, Stanley Hagler, Elsa Schiaparelli, Coco Chanel—the list goes on. Contemporary designers are avidly collected as well: Bob Mackie, Joan Rivers, Wendy Gell, Lawrence Vrba, and David Mandell all have ardent followers.

COLLECTOR'S COMPASS

Don't fall for the common misconception that bargains are not to be had from dealers who specialize in jewelry—many of your best purchases will be from the most knowledgeable dealers.

An even greater mistake is to assume that bargains abound in junk shops or that a good collection can be made up of bargains alone.

Some artists, famous for their work in other media, also designed jewelry. For instance, collectors of the celebrated glass art of René Lalique eventually want examples of his jewelry.

Manufacturer

Some collectors buy only Trifari, for example, or Coro; others purchase examples from many manufacturers, but group them by company for display.

Because most of the biggest costume jewelry companies were in business for decades and were quite prolific, just attempting to collect everything made by one company could take a lifetime—and amount to a very large collection.

Material

Numerous people plan their acquisitions by material, defining their collections broadly (say, any ornament that is pure gold or set with jade) or narrowly (gold cufflinks from the 1930s, for instance, or hand-carved African zebrawood pieces).

Many people who collect according to some other criterion actually organize their collections by materials: all plastics together, all Mexican silver, all ceramic beads, for instance.

Motif

Many collectors concentrate on motifs, searching out examples of mesh bracelets, charm bracelets, or Maltese Cross brooches. A second-generation jewelry collector narrowed her specialty to articulated silver charms with enameling whose motifs fit categories such as holidays.

Motifs are the most common lure for people who originally have no intention of becoming collectors. They begin searching for a favorite image—teddy bears, Christmas trees, roses—and soon realize that the majority of their finds, and the ones they can wear, are jewelry. Voila! Another collection is born!

Theme

Still other collectors seek items by theme, collecting, for example, military jewelry or ballet-themed pieces.

A variation on theme is to collect *occasional* or promotional pieces. One such collectible is Thief of Baghdad jewelry, issued as a tie-in with the great 1940 movie of the same name, produced by Alexander Korda. Its flamboyant "Arabian Nights" style made it an exotic standout at the time, a quality that holds enduring appeal for a select group of collectors even today.

Movie tie-in: *Thief of Baghdad* brooch

Technique

Yet another popular unifying principle for collecting and displaying vintage jewelry is according to the technique (or sometimes combination of methods) used to make it.

There are endless variations: one collector may include every fine enameled piece she can locate; another may choose only cloisonné earrings, or Art Nouveau plique-à-jour. Others collect examples of surface embellishment—embossing, engraving, etching, married metals, inlay, lamination, granulation—while a handful restrict their collections to mother-of-pearl inlay or delicate wire filigree.

Series

Sometimes, jewelry is collected in a series. For example, when Alfred Phillipe was the head designer for Trifari, he designed a series called Moghul (1949). It consisted of eighteen pieces of gold-plated sterling, set with rhinestones in jewel tones. The glass stones were molded in a style known as "fruit salad." Lucky is the collector who can assemble the entire Moghul series!

Sets

One goal shared by most jewelry collectors is to assemble an entire set of something. No one knows why some people break up a beautiful set, or *parure*, of jewelry. But once a collector owns a lovely necklace by a great designer, the search is usually on to find the earrings, bracelet, brooch, and, perhaps, even a ring, to complete the set.

Like Items

A significant number of people collect only one type of jewelry—such as lockets, or tie tacks, or earrings—usually refining the criteria to narrow the range somewhat.

Even more collectors combine like items for the purpose of storage or display, keeping all the brooches together and the bracelets with other bracelets. One expert collector further arranges her items by color, allowing her to dress a little more quickly, as she can see all the blue bracelets at once. She frequently mixes pieces by different designers—even those made of different materials—because they simply look stunning together!

Hearts interpreted in a charming variety of styles

Period Jewelry

Many collectors focus on jewelry from the period surrounding a historic event, such as the Civil War. Others concentrate on collecting any jewelry made during a defined stylistic era, such as Georgian, Victorian, or Art Deco.

One authority we interviewed set out to collect a few outstanding examples from each era and artistic style, beginning in the early 1700s! Highly selective, she has amassed a collection that ranges from glamorous Georgian pieces through early-, mid- and late-Victorian examples; includes Art Nouveau, Arts and Crafts, Art Deco, and Art Retro; and continues with distinctive contemporary jewelry.

Value and Price Trends

Jewelry collecting has truly hit its stride. It is a well-established collectible, but different specialties keep elbowing their way into the limelight, providing the excitement necessary to keep the hobby appealing.

The collectibles market is affected by news, so values rise or fall depending on what people hear. Auctions at which some rare pieces realize record prices can impact values broadly. One example: a bracelet made of different colors of Bakelite sold at a recent auction for more than $20,000. The market reacted by pumping up prices for the better pieces, while prices for more common pieces actually fell. In general, prices for antique jewelry increased 20% to 30% each year in the 1990s.

Prices can range from 25 cents to many thousands of dollars. Common brooches with colored rhinestones generally sell in the $25 range. Those signed by famous designers may command up to $500, while a piece by Lalique may sell for several thousand dollars. The more in demand a piece of jewelry is, the more elevated its pedigree, the finer its condition—the higher the price.

COLLECTOR'S COMPASS

Never set out to collect as an investment—it's an enterprise doomed to failure. Yes, a small fraction of collectors do make a fortune when they sell, but the odds are little better than playing the lottery.

If you collect what you like, learn everything there is to know about it, build and develop an excellent collection, then the likelihood is that its value will steadily appreciate.

Prices in some jewelry categories are high, and some jewelry that enjoyed high prices in previous years has now dropped in value. These conditions are due in part to the Internet having made the market global. Collectors are able to go to an online auction and see for themselves how many examples of a particular piece may be for sale at a given time, as well as prices realized in recent completed auctions. As a result, many items that were thought to be rare are now perceived to be fairly common, and prices for those items have dropped. You will soon discover that the more you learn about your collectible, the easier it is to decide what you are willing to pay.

There are still many opportunities to buy low and sell high. It happens every day. A collection of antique, heirloom, or collectible jewelry is very likely to appreciate over the next ten or twenty years, as new collectors discover it, and it becomes scarcer. As collectors become more sophisticated, the better examples will increase sharply in value and the lower end of the spectrum will decrease. Those items in the middle will likely hold their value or increase slightly.

American fashion jewelry production by the great houses has come to an end. That's a big chunk of the market that will be drying up shortly. Quality contemporary designer jewelry by Vrba, Mandell, Sorrell, Moini, and St. Gielar will fill the gap.

There are several specialized jewelry auctions held throughout the year at all levels, from Sotheby's and Christie's to the smallest country auction house, as well as on the Internet.

Specialized jewelry and accessory shows are held regionally; and the biannual Vintage, Fashion and Costume Jewelry conventions are the culmination of various mini-conventions held all over the country throughout the year.

Collectors' groups often sponsor jewelry seminars on topics ranging from materials identification to how to spot reproductions. And most antiques trade papers and magazines now have jewelry columns.

As you can see, there are any number of resources for learning about your new avocation—a favorite pastime since Cleopatra got gussied up to meet Marc Antony. Jewelry is a collection that allows you to demonstrate your taste, interests, and personality, and to enjoy the thrill of the hunt as much as the treasure itself.

References and Suggested Reading

Antique Jewelry: A Practical and Passionate Guide by Rose L. Goldemberg
Jewels of Fantasy by Deanna Farneti Cera
One Hundred Years of Collectible Jewelry by Lillian Baker

ESSENTIAL BACKGROUND FOR JEWELRY COLLECTORS

The tradition of jewelry making is rich and dramatic. Every culture, during every era of civilization, has contributed jewelry-making materials, designs, and techniques. Not only is jewelry a universal art form, but it is also universally adored and collected—for intrinsic value, for religious significance, for sentiment, and for other reasons as unlimited as the imaginations of collectors.

A Bit of History

Asking who "invented" jewelry is a bit like asking who "invented" clothing, but we might credit the Sumerians, circa 3000 B.C., with being the fathers of modern jewelry making.

Shell cameo of the Greek goddess Athena called Minerva by Romans, c. 1865

The Sumerians originated many of the methods used today. When they began to produce wonderful gold jewelry by using such innovations as filigree (delicate wire openwork), their trading partners in Africa, Asia, and the Middle East were quick to absorb them.

From the earliest times, colorful gems that could be worked easily were imbued with the greatest value. Jewelry performed an unusually important spiritual function in Egyptian society, where turquoise, lapis lazuli, carnelian, agate, and coral were used lavishly in necklaces, head ornaments, and bracelets. As *lapidary* (the skill of gem cutting) developed, harder materials such as amethyst, ruby, sapphire, and diamond were introduced.

The art of the jeweler assumed overwhelming importance to society in Europe during the fourteenth through eighteenth centuries. Men and women of the aristocracy and the wealthy merchant class adorned themselves with garlands of gold chains encrusted with rubies, pearls, and sapphires. Both sexes wore rings on both hands, often several on each finger. Medallions were worn on clothing of velvets, silks, and furs. The need to display increasingly impressive jewels had goldsmiths, silversmiths, and lapidaries working feverishly to meet the demand.

Subsequent generations of jewelers have introduced metal alloys, developed new techniques, and experimented with all manner of organic and synthetic materials. No era, no culture, no single technology has a monopoly on the truly universal art of jewelry making. And virtually every type of jewelry known has been collected by someone, somewhere, arguably making jewelry the most universal collectible.

Some Important Parameters

One book obviously cannot cover thousands of years of collectible jewelry. The coverage will concentrate on popular categories of jewelry produced during the past 200 years, still widely available in secondary outlets. While brand-new jewelry certainly may be collectible (indeed, it may be made and marketed specifically for that purpose), this book will not attempt to guide you on purchases you may make in the primary market through studios or retailers.

This book will introduce you to the many delights that jewelry collecting has to offer. It will give you a useful overview of the field and its many areas of special interest. And it will provide extensive resources for further learning, tell you about simple repairs you can accomplish yourself, and teach you how to avoid common pitfalls.

First, some important definitions you'll encounter in the marketplace:

> **antique jewelry:** One hundred years is considered the cutoff by most international customs rules, so "antique" is used here to describe pre-1900 jewelry only. You need to know that at

sales and shows, you're likely to find almost anything bally-hooed as "antique"; that doesn't make it so!

collectible jewelry: Used to denote jewelry made in the last fifty years (currently, 1950 to the present), to distinguish it from "antique" or "heirloom" jewelry. This term also has more generic, inclusive meanings, depending on context: (1) any and all jewelry ever made that is desirable to a collector may be "collectible jewelry," and (2) popular, widely available jewelry that is not new.

costume jewelry: *Webster's* defines it as "inexpensive jewelry designed for wear with current fashions," but most collectors and dealers use the term to mean any jewelry that is not made of precious stones, gold, or platinum, regardless of age or price. "Costume jewelry" commonly refers to items mass-produced since the Industrial Revolution, but it may also be wholly or partly handmade.

fine jewelry: Handmade or machine-made items containing precious stones and made of gold, silver, platinum, or palladium. Usually characterized by elegance and refined workmanship.

heirloom jewelry: A term broadly applied to jewelry that's approximately 50 to 100 years in age, regardless of style. In short, jewelry that's less than antique.

gem: Gemstone that has been faceted, shaped, or polished to enhance its natural beauty. Value is judged by color, clarity, weight, durability, and quality of cut and polish. Traditionally, the precious gems are diamond, ruby, sapphire, and emerald. All others are considered *semiprecious.* You will undoubtedly encounter the terms, and they are still widely used, but the distinction between precious and semiprecious has come under attack as artificial and unhelpful. The Gemological Institute of America no longer considers the terms useful, preferring to distinguish only between *natural* and *synthetic* stones. Thus, a fine specimen of garnet or opal may be worth far more than a so-so diamond.

gemstone: Naturally occurring rough material from which gems are fashioned. Usually mineral (diamond, emerald), but

continued on page 24

JEWELRY STYLES AND CHARACTERISTICS

Period	Characteristics	Museum/Gallery Collections
Georgian, 1714–1837	Glamorous, imaginative, delicate, and light; more austere and dignified after 1775; generous use of rubies, sapphires, emeralds, gold	Peabody Essex Museum, Salem, Mass. Museum of Fine Arts, Boston; Cooper-Hewitt National Design Museum, New York; National Museum of American History, Smithsonian Institution, Washington, D.C.; Walters Art Gallery, Baltimore
Early Victorian, 1837–1860	Romantic, sentimental, nostalgic; often celebrates memory of person or animal, a commemorative date, image of a sweetheart; lockets, chatelaines	Bennington Museum, Bennington, Vt. Fleming Museum, Burlington, Vt. Pine Forest Historical Museum, Edmore, Mich. Greenfield Village, Dearborn, Mich. Victoria and Albert Museum, The British Museum, London
Mid-Victorian, 1860–1885	Grand, forthright, assertive, and solid with a bold look; lots of mourning jewelry, black stones—jet, French jet, onyx; quantity and variety make it easy to collect	Museum of Fine Arts, Boston; J. Paul Getty Museum, Malibu, Calif. Indiana University Museum, Bloomington, Ind. Metropolitan Museum of Art, New York; University of Pennsylvania Museum, Philadelphia; Walters Art Gallery, Baltimore; Providence Jewelers' Museum, Providence, R.I.
Late Victorian/ Edwardian, 1885–1905	Aesthetic, lighter in scale, dainty; stars, crescents, bird motifs, Japanese designs; alexandrite, amethyst, garnet, moonstone, opal, sapphires, platinum; heavily influenced by Alexandra, wife of Edward VII	Cooper-Hewitt National Design Museum, Metropolitan Museum of Art, New York; Smithsonian Institution, Washington, D.C.; Victoria and Albert Museum, The British Museum, London

JEWELRY STYLES AND CHARACTERISTICS

Period	Characteristics	Museum/Gallery Collections
Art Nouveau, 1895–1910	Sensuous, emotionally beautiful; stylized motifs from nature with flowing lines, female forms, no sharp angles; artistry in design and composition emphasized; cabochons, ivory, sterling, enameling favored	Metropolitan Museum of Art, New York; Walters Art Gallery, Baltimore; Musee des Arts Decoratifs, Paris; Calouste Gulbenkian Museum, Lisbon
Arts and Crafts, 1880–1920	Strong lines, controlled movement; interlacing, complex motifs; design more disciplined than Art Nouveau, with emphasis on handwork: hammering, etching, embossing, patination, brass, copper, sterling	The American Craft Museum, New York; Le Musee de Arts Decoratifs de Montreal, Quebec; Renwick Gallery, Washington, D.C.
Art Deco, 1920–1930	Streamlined, with concise, angular lines in strong geometric patterns; abstracts, "Machine Age" designs executed in synthetic and natural gemstones with plated metals and plastics	Providence Jewelers' Museum, Providence, R.I. Cooper-Hewitt Museum, New York
Art "Retro," 1935–1945	Extravagantly massive; pinkish-colored metals and baguette stones popular; stylized scrolls, floral motifs, brickwork, honeycomb and other geometrics; exaggerated use of genuine and synthetic colored gems with small diamonds as accents; sterling, Lucite, Bakelite	No known museum collections

continued from page 21

sometimes rock (jade, lapis lazuli) or an organic product (pearl, amber, jet). The general term "gemstone" is now commonly used in place of the outdated "precious" and "semi-precious" distinctions.

period jewelry: An inexact term, usually applied to fine jewelry, to describe that a piece is old—usually 50 to 100 years of age. The term becomes more useful when it's coupled with a descriptive name that indicates the time frame or relates to a style, such as Victorian or Art Nouveau.

synthetic gemstones: Stones created in the laboratory to be chemically, optically, and physically identical to their natural counterparts. Man-made gemstones have many practical uses, only one of which is to masquerade as cut-and-polished gems set into jewelry.

vintage jewelry: A term often applied to costume jewelry to describe a piece that's less than an antique, in other words, less than 100 years old. It's often used with a descriptive term indicating a period, style, or type of jewelry, such as "1930s vintage," "vintage Art Deco," or "vintage costume," though it may be used alone.

Categories and Styles

There are literally hundreds of categories and individual styles of jewelry, each deserving its own book. So, this section will briefly introduce you to the broad category of mass-produced costume jewelry, then discuss two important style movements of the last 150 years. From there, our expert contributors suggest the best books, videos, and collectors' clubs to help you pursue in-depth study of particular eras, designers, or styles.

Costume Jewelry

What materials are used?

Costume jewelry can be made of almost anything—wood, plastic, beads, bones, shell, lava, glass, sterling silver plated with gold, base metal plated with gold, pot metal, human hair, horse hair. The only thing it can't be made of, by definition, is diamonds, rubies, emeralds, or other precious stones.

How is it made?

Costume jewelry is made by many processes. It can be handmade or machine made. It can be partly handmade and partly machine made. Many manufacturers of costume jewelry produced both handmade and machine-made pieces, sometimes in the same factory. A good illustration of this is the different techniques used to set rhinestones.

Hand-set rhinestones are individually placed into a pronged setting, and the prongs are bent over the stone to secure it. This is the same method used to set gemstones. Machine-set stones are easily identified by the metal strip running behind the pronged cups. These cups are actually threaded onto the strip. A machine then sets a stone into each cup and simultaneously folds the prongs over the stone. Hand-set pieces usually sell for more money than the machine-set ones.

Materials and techniques affect collectibility and price. Just as hand-set stones sell for more, Austrian crystal stones command higher prices than modern American glass stones. Pieces made of sterling silver command higher prices than gold- or silver-plated pieces. Rhodium-plated items and gold-plated sterling are also highly prized.

What is its condition?

Sterling silver, rhodium plate, and Bakelite are fairly durable, though subject to wear with longtime use. Bakelite can craze, become dull and/or discolor with exposure to heat and/or strong sunlight. Plated metals, such as silver-plated pot metal or gold-plated base metal, are prone to losing their plating over time as well as cracking and peeling—regardless of use—unless they are carefully stored and protected. Excessive cleaning of plated metals will hasten the loss of plating, as well.

Rhinestones are prone to deterioration, evidenced as darkening, clouding, or dulling. This usually means that the foil backing of the stone has been damaged. Enamels can wear and peel off too, especially if they are not protected from rubbing against clothing. And once a mosaic loses even one tile, it is doomed. That one missing tile will loosen the others, and they'll all begin to fall out. Never buy a mosaic with missing tiles.

How was it originally identified?

Some early costume jewelry wasn't signed. Even designers with strong reputations didn't always sign their work. Miriam Haskell jewelry was unsigned until the early fifties. It is well known that Schreiner made as many unsigned pieces as signed ones. This poses a problem, especially for beginning collectors. You must learn to recognize the work of a favorite designer before acquiring any unsigned pieces which, in general, will sell for less than comparable signed pieces.

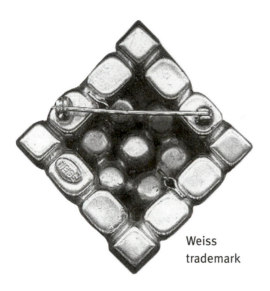

Weiss
trademark

Some manufacturers, such as Trifari, always sign pieces, using an incised trademark. Others used a signature on an applied plaque at the back of each piece. Still others attached a tiny tag to necklaces and signed those. In general, the earlier the piece, the less likely it is to have an attached tag.

Much costume jewelry was originally sold at house parties, which is how Sarah Coventry jewelry was sold. Most was sold through department stores and boutiques, with advertising appearing in leading women's magazines. In general, except for presentation boxes, packaging was up to the store, so it wasn't "original."

Some designers used a numbering or dating system. Marcel Boucher items (MB, Boucher, Marboux) are usually numbered. Hollycraft jewelry is both signed and dated with the year of manufacture, a decided boon to collectors. Numbers can be obtained from original catalogs.

Design patent numbers and copyright symbols may help reveal when the design of a piece originated. They don't, however, tell you when the specific piece was manufactured.

Patents could be obtained by jewelry makers for both mechanical innovations—such as the devices on Coro Duettes that allow two dress clips to be fastened together and worn as one brooch—as well as the aesthetic designs themselves. But design patents were difficult to obtain—requiring a lengthy and complicated application process. Pieces carrying a number preceded by "Des. Pat." or just "D" have been design patented. Some design patent numbers are not so designated. Some makers marked their designs "patent pending" (or "pat. pend.").

The Patent and Trademark Office has a Web site, www.uspto.gov, where you can find further information on design patents and link to a list of issue years and patent numbers for both design and mechanical patents. While design patent numbers began with "1" they don't begin showing up on costume jewelry until sometime in the 1930s, when they were already into five digits; the sequence went into six digits in 1936.

Some manufacturers—Coro among them—began to use the copyright symbol after it was introduced in 1947 to discourage copies, but without formal registration with the U.S. Copyright Office. Makers of knockoffs were evidently savvy to that fact, and copying continued until Trifari brought action for copyright protection for its designs, which was granted in 1954. Thereafter, few manufacturers continued with the arduous patent application process, and most resorted to registering their design copyrights and marking their designs with the copyright "©" and the year. It is interesting to note that some designs, probably because they weren't patented or copyrighted, were manufactured by more than one company. One example is a brooch called "The Chinaman," which was signed by both Har and Napier.

Hollycraft
trademark

Art Nouveau

Naturalistic motifs—flowers, leaves, and animals—were popular in jewelry designs on both sides of the Atlantic throughout the nineteenth century. But it wasn't until 1895, with the opening of Samuel (a.k.a. Siegfried) Bing's Parisian interior decor gallery, *Maison de l'Art Nouveau*, that the highly stylized interpretations of nature that came to be called Art Nouveau were first unveiled in jewelry design, among many other decorative arts. Two fine references about the style are Dr. Joseph Sataloff's *Art Nouveau Jewelry* and Vivienne Becker's *Art Nouveau Jewelry*.

What elements distinguish the style?

The Art Nouveau style is sensuous, with a feel of fantasy and magic. It was a huge change from the rigid and somber Victorian

Art Nouveau brooch

Art Nouveau locket

Art Nouveau ring

These pieces exhibit the sense of organic motion typical of Art Nouveau jewelry.

style of jewelry. It represented a revolution in taste, a rebellion against the Industrial Revolution, and, many experts believe, a rebellion against Victorian mores.

A characteristic feature of Art Nouveau is composition: airy, imaginative, charming, an expression of design freedom. It makes use of flowing line, continuously bending in circular modulations, often called the "whiplash curve." The emphasis is on artistry. The settings are not there to provide a showcase for gemstones; they are to be admired for themselves.

What materials were used?

Yellow gold was the preferred metal for compositions, but silver, silver plate, copper, and filled gold were used to excellent effect. Emphasis was on soft pastel colors that blended into one another. Favorite stones were pearls, opals, moonstones, and rock crystal. If diamonds were used, they were small and accented the design, not used as a focal point. You'll find examples with ivory, shell, steer's horn, tortoise shell, molded glass, pâte de verre, and pastel enamels.

In England, the emphasis was placed on the "craft" rather than on artistic expression, probably because of the strong Arts and Crafts movement. In France, jewelers' handmade items had a carved effect, like sculpture, that gave pieces perspective. This French style Art Nouveau is the most recognized. Smooth, polished stones were used to highlight the design of the setting and to improve composition.

Arts and Crafts

How did the style develop?

The Arts and Crafts movement began in 1860s England as a reaction against the "dehumanizing machine." Artists formed guilds, living and working communally in an effort to bring art to the common people. There was a conscious effort to create beautiful pieces from inexpensive materials, which were chosen for color, finish, and texture rather than value.

What are its hallmarks?

Composition was stylized, utilizing strong lines with controlled movement and interlocking, complex motifs.

Design was more disciplined than Art Nouveau, and executed primarily in silver or brass with *cabochons* (gems cut without facets). Opal, moonstone, and turquoise were preferred over more ostentatious gems. All forms of enameling used bright colors. "Unglamorous" materials were favored.

Typical motifs were based on medieval sources and Celtic revival themes. Arts and Crafts jewelry also featured many of the nature themes popular in Art Nouveau.

Designers and Manufacturers

Designers are usually considered the more important criterion by collectors—unless, of course, you collect by manufacturer. There are a number of excellent books recommended later in this section that provide great detail on the most "collectible" designers, with information on the companies they worked for and how their work was signed or dated. Because there are so many books that cover the histories of major U.S. and European manufacturers, we will tell just one fascinating story here.

The Eisenberg Company of Chicago was founded in 1914 to manufacture upscale ladies' ready-to-wear fashions. During the 1930s, the company designed and commissioned rhinestone jewelry to go with its clothes; indeed, some of these items were permanently affixed to the garments.

Customers loved the brooches and clips. In fact, they loved them more than they loved the clothes and asked to buy the jewelry, but the Eisenbergs would not sell it separately. The result? Jewelry began to "walk" out of stores. At last, the Eisenberg family realized that there was an opportunity in all this, and they began a separate costume jewelry division. It wasn't long before they abandoned clothing altogether, becoming one of the foremost costume jewelry houses in the world.

Today, the Eisenberg Company is still in business, headed by Karl Eisenberg, grandson of the founder. The company has reissued many of those classic designs from the thirties. Eisenberg jewelry has always been lauded for its high-quality materials and workmanship. The Eisenbergs used many manufacturers—and kept them a secret—as did all the costume jewelry houses.

Frequently, these jobbers would produce additional pieces of a client's design and sell them, unsigned. This is why every serious collector of costume jewelry has had the experience of finding an exact duplicate of some well-known designer piece, identical in every way, except for the missing signature.

The Best Sources for a Quick Education

Our expert contributors put their heads together to come up with a "short list" of the premier resources you can use to get a crash course in jewelry collecting. There are many valuable references on specialized topics listed in each section and at the end of the book, but the club newsletters, books, and videos listed here will give you an excellent general background.

Collector's Clubs

Jewelcollect is an online e-mail mailing list server. It was founded and is still run by Isabelle Bryman, proprietor of Liz Collectible Jewelry (www.lizjewel.com) and the Costume Jewelry Guide for About.com. Members sign up at the club's Web site.

Jewelcollect's membership increases daily. Members send queries to the group, comment on recent purchases or auctions, use the site's bulletin board to list items they have for sale or want to buy, and ask for advice on such topics as jewelry repair and Web-site development. Several authors of books about costume jewelry belong to this group. Jewelcollect members also hold an annual auction of costume jewelry and donate the proceeds to a specific charity. Membership is free. Simply go to www.jewel collect.org and follow the instructions.

Vintage, Fashion, and Costume Jewelry (VFCJ) is a club run by Lucille Tempesta. A quarterly newsletter contains features that examine different categories of jewelry in depth, with beautiful color photos. The newsletter also carries news about the collectible jewelry world and classified ads from buyers and sellers. Many members contribute by writing essays.

Every other year, the club holds a national convention in Providence, Rhode Island, the historical center of the world's costume jewelry industry. In the off years, regional conferences are held. Membership, which includes four issues of the newsletter, costs $20 per year. To join, write to Lucille Tempesta, care of VFCJ, P.O. Box 265, Glen Oaks, NY 11004.

The American Society of Jewelry Historians is dedicated to the scholarly pursuit of jewelry history, from ancient to modern. It is a nonprofit organization.

The society's frequent lectures are held in New York City and the surrounding area, so it best serves members who live in the area. A quarterly newsletter lists events and exhibits of interest in the United States and abroad. It also features important educational articles and provides summaries of presentations and lectures. Membership information can be obtained from 1333A North Avenue, P.O. Box 103, New Rochelle, NY 10804; (212) 744-3691.

Seminars and Courses

The annual Antique and Period Jewelry and Gemstone Conference, held at Bryant College, Smithfield, Rhode Island, includes a two-day preconference called "Jump Start," which is geared specially for beginners. You can obtain information on enrollment by contacting the conference director, Joyce Jonas, at 212-535-2479 or by logging on to www.jonas4jewelry.com.

The West Coast Antique and Period Jewelry Seminar is held annually in Southern California. For information, contact its director, Christie Romero, at the Center for Jewelry Studies, P.O. Box 424, Anaheim, CA 92815 (714-778-1828) or cr4jewelry@aol.com.

Gemology and jewelry workshops are conducted by Judith Fineblit Anderson, owner of Bijoux Extraordinaire. The workshop series is presented in Manchester, New Hampshire. Call 603-624-8672 or e-mail judi@jewelryexpert.com.

Both the National Association of Jewelry Appraisers at P.O. Box 6558, Annapolis, MD 21401-0558 (301-261-8270) and the International Society of Appraisers at Riverview Plaza Office Park, 16040 Christensen Road, Suite 102, Seattle, WA 98188-2965 (206-241-0359) or www.isa-appraisers.org offer antique and period jewelry courses.

Trade Papers and Specialty Publications

Antique Trader
P.O. Box 1050
Dubuque, IA 52001
A weekly trade paper available by subscription only. It carries classified ads by people who want to buy or sell. A good resource, but act fast—the best items get snapped up quickly.

Auction Forum USA
341 West 12th Street
New York, NY 10014
Information on auction contents, locales, and results.

Gemological Institute of America
The Robert Mouawad Campus
5345 Armada Drive
Carlsbad, CA 92008
Technical information and publications; seminars in gemology and lapidary techniques.

Kassoy
32 West 47th Street
New York, NY 10036
Modern equipment information for gemologists and lapidaries.

Modern Jeweler
P.O. Box 2939
Shawnee Mission, KS 66201
Up-to-date information on contemporary jewelry, including reproductions and new collectibles.

Precious Metals Institute
5 Mechanic Street
Attleboro, MA 02703
Offers general, as well as industrial, information about precious metals.

Books

There are so many excellent books, most lavishly illustrated, that it's tough to choose just a few. Because the market is constantly fluctuating, it's wise not to depend on the values listed in price guides. Nonetheless, a number of price guides contain history and background information that's hard to find elsewhere, so several are included among the must-haves. For complete annotated citations of the following references, see "Resources to Further Your Collecting."

Antique and 20th Century Jewellery, 2nd ed., by Vivienne Becker. Make this a must for your library. Each chapter concentrates on one topic, but it's easy to find information without having to read the entire book. It has great illustrations and cross-referencing.

The Bakelite Collection by Matthew L. Burkholz. A beautiful book that visits collectors who got in on the ground floor and have stunning collections. You'll see things you never dreamed existed.

Collecting Rhinestone and Colored Jewelry, 4th ed., by Maryanne Dolan. There's an extensive section on trademarks to help you identify and date jewelry. All the photos are in black and white.

A Collector's Guide to Costume Jewelry: Key Styles and How to Recognize Them, by Tracy Tolkien and Henrietta Wilkinson. Lives up to its title and more. It also has historical information. Great color photography and line drawings.

Costume Jewelers: The Golden Age of Design by Joanne Dubbs Ball. Organized by designer, this book will allow you to concentrate on your favorites, learning the bios and company histories of the best and brightest. Beautiful photos.

Costume Jewelry Identification and Price Guide by Harrice Simons Miller. A favorite of our expert contributors. You'll want to disregard the pricing because it's probably out-of-date, but there's so much background information that you're sure to learn all about your area of interest. All photos are in black and white.

European Designer Jewelry by Ginger Moro. If you thought all costume jewelry originated in the United States, you'll get an education here. A weighty tome with gorgeous color photos, arranged by country. This book is a work of art.

Jewels of Fantasy by Deanna Farneti Cera. If you don't think costume jewelry is art, you will after you look at the photos in this book. Essays by some of the foremost authorities in the field.

Old Costume Jewelry: 1870–1945 by Lynn Sallee. Information gathered from books, catalogs, magazine and newspaper articles, then organized in a concise manner.

One Hundred Years of Collectible Jewelry by Lillian Baker. Covers jewelers' merchandise (hatpins, handbags) as well as jewelry. Excellent glossary.

Victorian Jewellery by Margaret Flower. Hard to find, but probably the most definitive book on Victorian jewelry; indispensable for the beginner and expert alike.

Warman's Jewelry, 2nd ed., by Christie Romero. A good general reference. All photos are in black and white, except for a small center section, but this is a scholarly work with great historical information covering fine and costume jewelry from Georgian through modern studio work.

Videos

The Antique and Collectible Jewelry Video Series, Volumes I and II. C. Jeanenne Bell, noted author and lecturer, is most authoritative on Edwardian, Art Nouveau, Art Deco, and Victorian jewelry, contained in Volume I. After you've watched this video, you'll have a strong foundation in these specialties. Well made and educational.

Fabergé: Imperial Jeweler from A&E's Biography Series. The story of an artist whose priceless masterpieces continue to captivate people worldwide. Available from A&E Home Video Catalog #14123. Look for videotapes in this series on Cartier and Tiffany as well.

Hidden Treasures: A Collector's Guide to Antique and Vintage Jewelry of the 19th and 20th Centuries from Venture Entertainment Group, Inc. A fun, informative video hosted by Christie Romero, noted lecturer on jewelry collecting and author of *Warman's Jewelry.* Production values aren't great, but the jewelry is.

Study the Best Examples

An enjoyable and rewarding way to educate yourself in a variety of jewelry styles is to see the finest examples available. There are excellent exhibits of jewelry from many eras at the Boston Museum of Fine Arts, the Metropolitan Museum of Art and the Cooper-Hewitt in New York City, the Walters Art Gallery in Baltimore, and the Smithsonian Institution museums in Washington, D.C. Other galleries and museums have collections of one or more styles (see the Jewelry Styles and Characteristics chart on pages 22–23 for listings of museum and gallery collections).

Watch your local newspaper for touring exhibits passing through your area. When you travel, check the museums along your itinerary. Galleries, historical societies, and even libraries often have collections as a result of a bequest or regional proximity to an important designer or manufacturer.

High-end auction houses schedule previews that provide the opportunity to see—and even handle—excellent examples of antique and period jewelry. You need not be a registered bidder to attend the preview. Watch for auction announcements in your local newspaper or antiques and collectibles trade papers.

Web Sites

Costume Jewelry Collecting at About.com at costumejewels. about.com. This is the site where you can learn almost everything about costume jewelry. Guide Isabelle Bryman, who also runs Jewelcollect, provides fresh information each week, while maintaining extensive archives and hundreds of links to jewelry sites.

Jewelcollect at www.jewelcollect.org. This site is the key portal to the world of costume jewelry online, as it contains links to some of the major jewelry dealers on the Internet, those sites have links to other jewelry sites, and so forth. Also, there's a link to the Jewelcollect message board, where members post items for sale, items wanted, and other information.

You can also join Jewelcollect's e-mail mailing list server here. More than five hundred members discuss all sorts of jewelry topics, and questions from beginners are both welcomed and encouraged. Just be prepared for a large volume of e-mail.

Morningglory at www.morninggloryantiques.com. A professionally run business and a beautiful collection that reflects the
well-edited taste of the proprietor.

A Wink and a Smile at www.wink.smile.com. Once you know
enough to tell the good stuff from the junk, here's where you'll
want to shop. This site has nothing but the best—exquisite
costume jewelry you won't see everywhere.

BEFORE YOU START COLLECTING

You're eager to begin collecting—but before you buy anything, be sure to learn as much as you possibly can. Let's begin with guidelines from collectors, dealers, and curators who tell you what they wish they'd known when they started out, as well as what they've learned through long—and sometimes painful—experience.

Ten Golden Rules of Collecting

1. Buy Only What You Like

The most important thing to remember when embarking on the road to a new collection—and it's also the rule most people leave by the wayside—is to buy only what you personally like.

It's sometimes easy to get caught up in the excitement of a rising market and be tempted to speculate. Don't buy items in which you have no real interest because you're betting that they'll appreciate in value.

Hollycraft rhinestone earrings, c. 1950

If you want a collection's value to appreciate, never regard buying as an investment only. One appraiser and gemologist says,

"The best collections have always had the strong imprint of the owner's taste. The worst collections are those on which money has been spent in the hope of a rising market. Buy what you like, concentrating on quality rather than quantity."

2. Learn All You Can First

Become an expert in what you love. Hit the library, read the books, go to shows, attend auctions, read catalogs. Do all of this before you buy anything. When you're well prepared, you'll enjoy the hunt—and the find—much more.

Novices (experienced collectors too!) often find themselves in a quandary due to misinformation. False statements are made all the time, either deliberately or through ignorance. Never depend on a single source. If you use multiple sources—books, magazines, trade papers, videos, other collectors—you'll quickly learn to spot errors and avoid expensive mistakes.

3. Look for Quality, Not Quantity

Quantity is often important to a novice collector. The appreciation of quality comes with experience. You'll be ahead of the game if you can concentrate on quality in the beginning stages of collecting. See the accompanying Collector's Compass (page 42) for the criteria that affect quality and value. Practice using them each time you evaluate a piece of jewelry; they'll soon become second nature to you.

Buy the best quality you can afford. You are better off buying one bracelet with outstanding workmanship than three mediocre ones. The items at the top of the market always hold their value, always look great, and always last. Quality never goes out of style.

4. Stay within Your Budget

If the cost of a piece you want is too high, budget for it and wait until you can afford to buy.

Keep your head in competitive situations, such as auctions. In the heat of bidding, it can be easy to forget your budget. Desire can overwhelm discipline. However, a specialized auction may provide the only opportunity to buy "the" piece of jewelry for a collection. Here are some tips our experts wish they'd had when preparing for their first auctions:

- Find out whether your competitor is a dealer or another collector. A dealer will probably be buying for resale and likely will not bid a piece up to its retail value. On the other hand, a collector buying for a personal collection may be stiff competition; you or she may end up paying a premium over retail market value to take home a "prize."

- Specialized auctions usually have catalogs. Obtain one beforehand and study it carefully. Be sure you understand all the jargon in statements of attribution, provenance, and description used by the auction house. Also, familiarize yourself with the terms and conditions of sale, especially buyer's premiums.
- Set guidelines for yourself. First, decide how badly you want a certain object. Second, set a price limit and *stick to it.*

5. Profit from Your Mistakes

Everyone makes mistakes. You will too, and some of them will be costly. Don't beat yourself up over it. If the item is something you like (remember rule #1) and you paid too much for it, just wear and enjoy it. If it's a fake, and you were fooled, learn from the experience—it will be much tougher for someone to pass off a fake to you the next time!

6. Join a Club

There's no better way to meet other collectors, get a free education, and gain access to jewelry that rarely comes on the market than by joining a group. It's usually inexpensive or even free to join. You'll be amazed at how generous and helpful old-timers are to newcomers. They'll offer advice, tell you where to look for items you're seeking, recommend the best books, and help you identify the jewelry you have.

7. Honor Your Commitments

Be straightforward and dependable. Pay on time, answer correspondence, and keep your appointments. Once people know they can rely on you, they'll bring you the best. If they know that your word is good, they'll make an effort on your behalf.

8. Be a Friendly Competitor

Share information and keep in touch. A friendly person is apt to get leads about an object for his collection from competitors who already own one like it. In turn, give leads to others. You'll have a lot more fun in the long run.

9. Develop Relationships with Dealers

Once you know your area of specialty, go to shows and meet dealers who sell what you collect. Stop by and tell them what you are seeking. Give them your phone number, take their cards, and call once in a while to ask whether they've found anything for you.

It takes time and effort to establish a relationship, but once a dealer knows you'll buy from her, she'll watch out for items that will interest you and show you things before anyone else sees them.

10. Once You Gain Experience, Help Someone Else

Just as someone (probably more than one someone) helped you, you must be willing to help beginners. Aside from being the right thing to do, it's the way to keep the hobby going and to ensure that the market remains healthy.

Know the Language of Jewelry Construction

Collectors must know the language of jewelry construction, not only to make a determination of quality but also to accurately describe and date a piece of jewelry. Two excellent books on jewelry techniques and materials are Oppi Untracht's *Jewelry Concepts and Technology* and Robert von Neumann's *Design and Creation of Jewelry*.

The first important steps are to identify the piece, look at the construction technique, and determine whether the object is what you first thought. A new collector of old jewelry is likely to base an approximate date on only one fact. All aspects of a piece of jewelry—including the design, motif, scale, construction techniques, and materials used—must be considered before determining a date.

A Step-by-Step Guide to the Marketplace

The quantity and quality of jewelry to be found—and at what price—will depend greatly on the venue. Also, it's reasonable to assume that an antique jewelry dealer at a high-end show will answer all your questions about his merchandise. On the other hand, it's folly to assume that you'll get knowledgeable help at a thrift shop or yard sale. Here's what to expect.

Garage, Yard, and Tag Sales

If you are patient, you can still find great jewelry at garage, yard, and tag sales. It takes endurance to make the rounds, but perseverance pays off.

For garage and yard sales, it's important to have a plan. Get your local paper on Thursday night or Friday, whichever is the big day for garage-sale ads. In some areas, garage-sale ads appear as early as Tuesday. Pinpoint the sales that sound good and mark them on your map. Plan to hit about five or six sales.

Read the ads for the wealthiest towns in your area. The richest people have the best stuff, and you want to go where the best stuff is. People who advertise "antiques and collectibles" usually will have high prices on their things. And stay away from sales whose ads are predominantly baby clothes and toys. Young families will not have accumulated much old jewelry. Watch for key phrases, such as "estate sale," "empty-nest moving sale," and "40-year accumulation."

Now, pack up everything you're taking with you and get it ready the night before. If the first sale on your route starts at 8 A.M., plan to be there by 7:30. If the ad says "No Early Birds," believe it and get there at 8:00.

You've arrived bright and early at the first sale with your loupe in hand (or around your neck on a long cord). You head straight for the old jewelry box standing on the first table.

While you're rummaging through the box, exchange pleasantries with the proprietor. Ask if

COLLECTOR'S COMPASS ™

FACTORS THAT *INCREASE* VALUE ARE:

- good condition
- sound construction
- original stones, original findings, original box
- fine design
- excellent workmanship
- uniqueness
- provenance
- identifying marks (makers' marks, designer signatures)
- pairs (a pair of bracelets has more than twice the value of one bracelet)
- an entire suite (more valuable than the sum of the individual pieces)
- demand greater than supply

FACTORS THAT *DECREASE* VALUE ARE:

- poor condition
- obvious solder and glue repairs
- missing or replacement parts
- loose or defective stones (cracked, chipped) or other defective decoration (e.g., chipped enamel)
- unwanted decorations, such as monograms
- absence of identifying marks
- poor design
- shoddy workmanship
- fragility
- supply is greater than demand—and everyone knows it

there is any other jewelry that hasn't been put out yet. You'll be amazed at how many people will go upstairs and bring back a box of better jewelry!

Sometimes, people will say they have better jewelry but are not planning to sell it now. Grab your address card, add "costume jewelry" or "Aunt Millie's jewelry," and give it to the owners. Tell them you'd appreciate the chance to see it if they ever decide to sell. Many times, you'll get a call on Monday morning!

If you find something of interest, grab it—even if you're not sure! You can always put it down later, but if you don't pick it up now, someone else will. If you find yourself with too much to carry, ask the owner where you can start a pile of stuff, somewhere no one else will touch it. Use the loupe to examine every piece for missing or darkened stones, chipped plating, broken pins, or other damage. Put back anything that's broken, unless you can fix it yourself or it's unusual enough to warrant the expense of repair.

As a rule, don't spend more than fifteen minutes at any one sale (exception: you've found the mother lode of all vintage jewelry). When you've made your decisions, return the rejects to their places, and approach the owner. If you've chosen quite a few pieces, ask for a quantity discount. If each item is priced, add it up in your head, and expect to get a 10% to 15% discount for buying the lot. If the owner just adds everything up with no discount, and you think it's still a good price, by all means, pay it. Thank the owner and wish him a great day and a profitable sale. Deposit your jewels in the tray or box you brought, and move on to the next sale!

As soon as you have the chance, place each item in its own Ziploc bag. You don't want delicate pieces banging against each other, causing the stones to fall out or scratching the finish.

Treasure Hunter's Kit

Here's what you should pack the night before you set out on your shopping adventure:

- **1OX jeweler's loupe**—an absolute *must,* available at jewelry supply houses or on the Internet
- small penlight flashlight
- your favorite jewelry reference book
- map marked with your route
- small Ziploc bags
- shallow box or tray
- pen or pencil and notebook
- printed or handwritten cards with your name, contact information, and what you're looking to buy
- plenty of cash in small bills, preferably lots of singles
- baby wipes

By the second or third sale, you'll probably want to clean your hands with the baby wipes. This is dirty work. By the time you reach the fifth or sixth sale, it should be almost noon, and time to quit for the day.

Sometimes in your Saturday morning travels, you'll pass a sale you didn't know about along the way, one that looks promising from the road. Go ahead and stop! If the sale is unadvertised, there may be far less competition for your favorite things. Take a quick glance around. If you don't see any jewelry, ask the owner or leave.

Tag sales are a little different than garage or yard sales. They are usually run by a tag-sale company, an outside group brought in to organize, price, tag, and advertise the sale. These sales usually require you to line up at the crack of dawn to get a number. The lower your number, the earlier you get to go in. However, local dealers may have been through the merchandise long before you even heard about the sale. That's why it's important to establish a relationship with the tag-sale manager. You can do this by attending her sales frequently and inquiring about jewelry every single time. Keep leaving your name and phone number and keep buying jewelry at her sales. One of these days, she's going to call and invite you to preview the jewelry.

At most of these sales, the manager offers you the jewelry at the price marked. You have the option of paying the marked price or offering a lower bid. If the item remains unsold at the end of the sale, the manager will contact you about your bid. Other people may have left bids, and the highest bidder gets the jewelry.

Several experts advise that your best bet for finding great antique jewelry is a tag sale—rather than a garage or yard sale—in most areas of the country.

Flea Markets and Bazaars

Jewelry can be found at flea markets and bazaars, but remember that there is usually no control, no jurying of the merchandise. People can sell anything they choose. Some of it is fake. Much of it is junk. Be discerning. Examine everything closely, and try to see the object as it is, rather than as you would like it to be.

Arrive at the flea market early, while some of the dealers are still setting up. Talk to them; they'll bring pieces for you if they know you'll be back every Sunday. If you don't see what you want, ask for it. Some of the dealers will remember what you like and try to find it for you. Don't be disappointed if your efforts don't produce anything immediately—it takes time and persistence.

The opportunities for haggling are greater at flea markets than they are at garage sales. Most dealers expect haggling. Some even like it. This is a social environment and friendly banter will be returned with good humor. Expect a 10% to 15% discount—more if you're buying in large quantity.

Bazaars are usually held by churches, synagogues, and civic groups. Because the people doing the pricing don't always know the value of the items, these can be sources of great jewelry bargains. Everything is priced to move and bring in some money for charitable works. Don't ask for a discount at a charity bazaar (although occasionally you may be offered one by a good-natured volunteer if you buy a lot of stuff). If you know anyone on the bazaar committee, tell her what you buy, and ask her to keep an eye out for it. Most people will be glad to put something aside for a friend, especially if you are a good customer who buys regularly.

Thrift and Consignment Shops

First, there's the charity thrift shop, which usually has a professional appraiser on the staff. Prices tend to be high. Again, if you make regular appearances, purchases, and inquiries, the staff will alert you when something of interest comes in.

For-profit secondhand and thrift shops usually have a lot of junk you have to wade through. Many collectors find that these are usually a waste of time. However, it may be different in your town, so scout around before you make a final judgment. Prices should be negotiable here (they usually aren't negotiable at charity thrift shops, although you can request that the person in charge consider lowering a price for you).

A consignment shop may be a good place to buy. It is also a good place to sell when you upgrade your collection, particularly if the shop has a reputation for selling jewelry.

Consignment shops charge a percentage of the selling price as their commission for handling seller's merchandise. Therefore, it is to their benefit to get the most they can for the seller. But they do need frequent inventory turnover, so don't hesitate to ask whether prices are negotiable. Be prepared to make a reasonable offer on the spot if the manager is willing to call the owner to negotiate.

Most consignment shops automatically reduce prices after a

given period of time to make way for new merchandise. If you're interested in an item, ask when the price will be reduced. Remember, though, that waiting can be risky. Other interested parties may come along or may be waiting for the price to come down just as you are.

Pawn shops are another great source of jewelry. They may have a seedy reputation, but most are fine. Simply ask whether there is any vintage, estate, or costume jewelry. A shop may have tons, and it will all be priced way below the market.

Estate Sales and Auctions

Despite the fancy term, "estate jewelry" is—simply put—used jewelry. It is not necessarily high quality, or even desirable, and should not automatically guarantee the seller a fancy price.

Sales advertised as "estate" do attract swarms of dealers, and you are competing for the same merchandise. This puts you at a distinct advantage. A dealer who is going to sell you a necklace for $50 can only pay about $25 for it. But $30 probably seems like a great price to you, and makes you an attractive customer to the merchant selling the necklace. The only advantage the dealer has is that the seller of the necklace knows that a dealer buys in quantity. So, the best thing you can do as a retail customer is demonstrate that you will buy in quantity.

Get to know the professional sellers of estates in your region. Ask about their sales in advance.

Antiques and Collectibles Malls

Antiques and collectibles malls are group shops where each area, sometimes each showcase, is rented from the owner by an individual dealer. The mall personnel manage the sales of the merchandise.

Some owners are selective about whom they invite into their mall; some are not. Some owners are strict about what is placed in booths in the mall, barring reproductions and fantasy items. They may also require dealers to put in time at the shop, helping to run it. Some dealers pay straight rent, while others pay rent plus a percentage of sales. In malls where the inventory is juried, where the owner bans such things as fakes and unidentified reproductions, the quality of the merchandise will be higher, and so will the prices.

Most malls have standard discount policies, but if you find something you want and the price is still too high, mall personnel will usually phone the dealer to convey your offer or request a further discount on your behalf. If the dealer won't accept your offer, he'll likely make a counter offer, and you can still make a deal. Some mall managers also keep a file of customers' wants so they can call you if something of interest comes in. You definitely want to register for that! And sometimes a dealer will leave his business cards in his booth. If he has the kind of jewelry you like, give him a call. Perhaps he'll sell to you directly and pass along the savings he realizes by not paying a commission to the mall owner.

Individual Antiques and Collectibles Shops

Antiques dealers are an odd lot. It's a calling that attracts those who march to the beat of their own drum. Many don't keep regular hours, and you may have trouble getting in to see that gorgeous Schreiner set in the window. Can you think of any other store where the hours posted on the door say "Wednesday & Friday—by chance"?

Jewelry for sale

You will find these shops listed in the yellow pages, trade papers, on the Internet, or in a directory such as *Maloney's Antiques and Collectibles Resource Directory*. The Associated Antiques Dealers of America, Inc., also publishes a membership directory for public use. Each listing describes the member's merchandise and whether the business is "open" or "by appointment."

Top-quality and rare pieces are likeliest to surface in specialized jewelry shops, so it's worthwhile to persevere. If the hours are erratic, keep calling and leaving messages. Eventually, you'll get a call back, especially if you mention something you want to buy.

Be extra friendly when dealing with independent shop owners. Most got into this business to be masters of their own destinies. Most appreciate some conversation, particularly if it's about antiques. Ask these people all your questions.

Prices in individual shops are negotiable, but don't expect a bargain every time. A typical discount is 10% to 15%. If you're looking at an Eisenberg bracelet and you know the market is soft at the moment, you may want to offer a lower bid—especially if it appears that the bracelet's been sitting a while. Sometimes the dealer will take it, sometimes he won't. It can't hurt to ask.

Don't forget to be appreciative, even if you can't reach an agreement. The next time you come in, the dealer may be willing to bend a little for you.

Antiques and Collectibles Shows

Shows afford the best opportunity to visit a variety of dealers with quality merchandise. Antique or vintage clothing and accessory shows will expose you to some of the rarer pieces of jewelry on the market. Large general shows with hundreds—sometimes thousands—of dealers will bring you into contact with dealers who have jewelry but don't specialize in it. (Most dealers wind up with things because the price is right, or because they're part of a larger lot.) Such dealers usually want to get rid of the jewelry at a modest profit, and will sometimes sell it far below market value in favor

COLLECTOR'S COMPASS™

It's smart to negotiate for a better price, but trying to get a reduced price by criticizing the merchandise is never a good idea. After all, what dealer is going to negotiate with someone who says, "That's a ridiculous price for this piece of junk!"?

Here are some examples of good negotiating tactics:

- "I'm willing to pay $X for an item in this condition."
- "It's really lovely, but prices are down right now because there's so much Eisenberg on the market."
- "I'm afraid I can't invest that much in one necklace."

of a fast turnover. So, if you come across a sports memorabilia booth with a tray of costume jewelry in the corner, pounce on it!

Specialized shows are more likely to produce spectacular finds than general shows. The Estate Jewelers Association of America sponsors an annual show in a major city such as Las Vegas, New York, or Los Angeles. Contact them at:

Estate Jewelers Association of America
209 Post Street, Suite 718
San Francisco, CA 94108
Phone: 800-584-5522
Phone: 415-834-0718
Fax: 415-834-0717
estate-jaa@aol.com

But don't despair if you can't travel a great distance. General antiques and collectibles shows are held in many cities. Almost every dealer in a general show will offer some old jewelry, and bargains can be found if you know your stuff.

There's a myth that dealers have plenty of time before the show opens to shop for merchandise themselves. Most are setting up their displays and are too pressed for time, so if someone tells you that the dealers "already bought all the good jewelry," don't believe it.

Many different kinds of organizations, such as humane societies, churches, and civic groups, sponsor antiques and collectibles shows as fund-raising events. Sponsored shows often provide opportunities—called *previews*—for patrons to buy before the show opens to the public.

Some outdoor shows are so enormous that you won't be able to cover the territory. If a show is a manageable size, start at one end and go up and down the aisles, stopping at any booth that displays jewelry. Remember, dealers who do not specialize in jewelry often have some and are willing to part with it at much lower prices than jewelry dealers.

Introduce yourself to every dealer who carries the type of jewelry you want. Some collectors find it worthwhile to have cards printed up with their address, telephone number, and a list of what they collect. Others wear T-shirts, signs, or hats that proclaim their interests. If you walk a show wearing a signboard that says "I buy

continued on page 65

Jewelry Photo Gallery

Italian artisans used tiny pieces of semiprecious stone, glass, and other materials to form astonishingly intricate micromosaics. Classical architecture was a favorite subject—and popular among Victorian tourists looking for souvenirs of Rome—but peasants, animals, and other subjects were also depicted. Once a tile, or tesserae, is lost from a piece, it's nearly impossible to replace.

Early Victorian Roman micromosaic, c. 1840

Mid-Victorian Micromosaic set, c. 1860, framed elaborately in gold

Pietra Dura

*Pietra dura (*hard rock *in Italian) involves inlaying semiprecious stones into a soft stone such as marble, usually black. The stones in well made pieces should fit tightly together.*

Pietra dura drop, c. 1920

Pietra dura brooch, c. 1880

Millefiore brooch, c. 1920–1930

Millefiore

Millefiore (from the Italian mille fiori, *a thousand flowers) is made by cross-cutting rods of colored glass.*

Victorian

Solid, grand styling and sentimental imagery are hallmarks of Victorian jewelry. Its diversity of style and wide availability make it easy to collect.

Top right: Mid-Victorian gold brooch with original box, c. 1860. It's rare to find a Victorian piece like this one complete with original packaging, and that rarity makes packaged pieces valuable to collectors. Right: Mid-Victorian pink coral brooch, c. 1880.

Mid-Victorian gold Indian-pitch brooch, c. 1870

Above: Mid-Victorian gold snake brooch, c. 1880. Above right: Early Victorian diamond and enamel brooch, c. 1840. Below right: Mid-Victorian blond tortoiseshell earrings, c. 1870. Popular in the Victorian era, genuine tortoiseshell is no longer used in jewelry due to conservation efforts. Burnt tortoiseshell smells like burning hair.

Late Victorian/Edwardian

The Edwardian period encompasses the reign of Edward VII of England (1901–1910). Elegant and generally lighter in weight and scale than Victorian jewelry, Edwardian pieces commonly feature platinum, pearls, diamonds, and filigrees.

Edwardian platinum, pearl, and diamond brooch

Etruscan Revival gold bar pin, c. 1890

Insect brooch, c. 1890. Insects were popular subjects of Edwardian design.

Gemstone cameo circled with gold and pearls, c. 1900

Art Nouveau

Nature themes are typical of Art Nouveau jewelry. Free-flowing, curving lines with asymmetrical motifs—such as intertwining floral patterns—are common. Butterflies, dragonflies, swans, peacocks, and ethereal human forms with sinuous lines of long, flowing hair were favorite images.

Novelty brooch, parrot figural, c. 1900.

Silver plique à jour brooch, c. 1920

Plique à jour

Plique à jour (letting in light in French) is an enameling technique in which powdered glass (the enamel) is fused into the openings of metal cloisonné wire. Because it has no backing, the enamel is translucent and somewhat resembles stained glass.

Pearls

Organic gemstones, pearls should be kept in their original packaging or stored in soft cloth.

Platinum and pearl earrings, c. 1910

Pearl necklace, c. 1950s

Seed pearl bar pin, c. 1900

Hand-painted portrait brooch, signed by the artist, c. 1870

Hand-painted portrait brooch, signed by the artist, c. 1870

Mid-Victorian painted porcelain pendant, c. 1880

Enamel on gold necklace, c. 1920

Enamel on gold brooch/pendant, c. 1910

Enamel Jewelry

In the enameling process, ground glass is made into a paste, applied to metal, and then fired in a kiln.

Enamel brooch, c. 1900

Platinum and diamond brooch with enameled flowers and green jade leaves, c. 1930s

Costume Jewelry

Costume jewelry covers a broad range of materials, manufacturing methods, and styles. Most collectors and dealers use the term to mean any jewelry that is not made of precious stones, gold, or platinum, regardless of age or price.

Apple Juice-colored Bakelite floral brooch, c. 1930

Queen Anne Bakelite cherry brooch, c. 1930

There are many ways to organize a jewelry collection.
Grouping pieces by color makes wardrobe coordination easy!

Figural

The figural category encompasses jewelry intended to represent a human figure or everyday thing. Favorite subjects include fairies, birds, leaves, flowers, and insects.

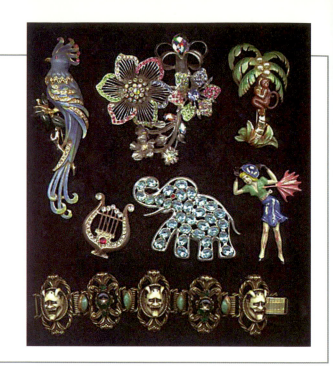

Designer Collections

Many collectors focus on just a few—or just one—designer or manufacturers, as shown by this grouping of Miriam Haskell pieces. One of the most collectible names in costume jewelry, Miriam Haskell began marketing jewelry in 1924 but did not begin signing her pieces until 1950.

Costume Jewelry

Schreiner brooches, above. Schreiner (1950s–1970) never manufactured jewelry in large quantities. Because they feature colorful designs and quality construction, Schreiner pieces are prized by collectors of costume jewelry.

Eisenburg (1914–present) started as a clothing manu-facturer, but the jewelry they made as accessories soon outstripped their garments in popularity. Above, a 1940 fur clip.

Coro Quivering Camelias Duette, c. 1940. Coro (1910–1979) sold pieces in every price range, from fifty cents to one hundred dollars, and produced an immense variety of jewelry.

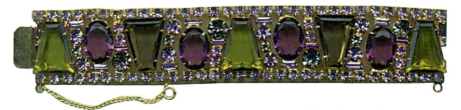

Alice Caviness rhinestone-and-glass bracelet, c. 1950. Vintage Caviness pieces might be somewhat scarce in the marketplace— they were originally available in high-end specialty shops.

Trifari sterling fur clip. Trifari (1918–present) jewelry, prized by many collectors, is known for outstanding design and construction.

Unsigned multicolored rhinestone set, sparkling with color, c. 1950.

Cococraft fighting fish, a piece that's become the subject of fakes. Authentic pieces like this one feature enameling that extends all the way to the fins, which should be closed at the tips.

continued from page 48

Victorian cameos," you can be sure that any dealer who carries them will stop you, either to show you some or to chat about what he has at home to sell.

Indoor shows are a little more reserved, but they're also likely to be smaller. Walk by each booth, glancing at what they have, and drop your card with dealers whose inventory looks promising.

If you see something you like, and the price is right, buy it! There's an old saying that goes, "The time to buy an antique is when you see it." You can mark down the booth number and plan to return after you've checked out the rest of the show, but if the item is exceptional, it probably won't be there when you get back. It is not reasonable to ask a dealer to hold something for you—unless you have paid for it. In other words, don't expect the dealer to remove a nice item and keep it from the eyes

Early Buying

Antiques and collectibles shows sometimes engage in an abhorrent practice called "Early Buying." For an additional, often exorbitant fee, you can enter the show hours earlier than the general admission and shop first.

Don't fall for this scam. The fee you pay goes directly into the show promoter's pocket. The dealers get none of this money, yet they are forced to be at the show three hours early. So, there they are—disgruntled, sleepy, and freezing at 5 A.M., knowing that they could sell you that Victorian jet brooch just as easily at 9 A.M. You—and other customers like you—have apparently been convinced by the promoter's advertising that $50 or $75 will net you some fabulous stuff that will all be gone before the show opens. Any dealer will tell you that he's never done a show in his life where all the good stuff was gone by the end of the show, much less by the time the doors opened.

of other collectors just so you can return later and say you really don't want it.

When you've been placed on a dealer's mailing list, he will often send you a postcard informing you of an upcoming show. Call ahead to find out whether he has anything in your area of interest. If so, he may offer to sell it to you immediately or hold it until you arrive at the show. If he sends the item on approval, you needn't send any money ahead of time. You need only examine the merchandise, make a decision, and either return it or send payment for it promptly.

Dealer Fixed-Price Catalogs and Auctions

Some dealers send out mail-order catalogs or run independent mail and telephone jewelry auctions. In theory, a fixed price is an honest price because it is the same for everyone. However, that doesn't make it a good value, so beware.

Our expert contributors advise that you stay away from these sales for the simple reason that jewelry should be carefully examined before you buy it. Virtually none of the mail-order lists come with photos. They have one-sentence descriptions with either a price or minimum bid. Condition is paramount in jewelry, yet the lists rarely mention the condition of the item for sale.

If you decide to do business this way, all you need to do is get on mailing lists. Local newspapers and trade papers all carry classified listings by dealers who sell this way. Simply drop them a postcard and you'll get the mailings. But proceed with caution.

These mailing-list dealers are becoming a rare breed. Most have given up this sales method in favor of doing business on the Internet.

Web Sites and Internet Auctions

The Internet offers advantages and disadvantages. On the plus side, you can view the item for sale and, depending on the quality of the photograph, learn almost everything you need to know about the piece. The seller is free to offer you lots of information or very little, and has 100% of your attention while doing it. Since we generally see what we want to see, however, it's important to be objective.

Ask every question you can think of before you make an offer for anything you see on the Internet. If the photo is fuzzy, ask for a better one. If the item's dimensions are missing, ask for them. Inquire in detail about the condition of the piece—and be specific. Ask if there are any missing stones, any cloudy or yellowing stones, any scratches or missing plating, or any missing parts, chips, or rough edges. Ask about the return policy, the shipping method, the shipping costs—in short, ask for anything that may be missing from the listing. If every single one of your questions is not answered to your satisfaction, or if a new and better photo does not arrive via e-mail, decline to buy the item.

Remember to review the auction rules before you bid in any online auction. If you are planning to bid on an item after asking about it, save the e-mails between you and the seller in case the item isn't up to snuff. There is an excellent article by Judith Katz-Schwartz about how to trade in online auctions. You can find it at www.msjudith.net/other/010199.htm.

eBay Jewelry Category Descriptions

When you first set out to buy through an Internet auction site, you may be confused by some of the categories. Sellers are free to list their items in any category they choose, so some categories contain unlikely listings. This can be the result of mistaken identification—or it can signal the seller's previous success at selling similar items by using that category. Below are the categories designated by the Internet auction site eBay and a description of what you'll find in each.

Ancient/Ethnographic: Vintage Egyptian or Egyptian Revival, tribal, Mideastern, Native American, Asian, and other jewelry with a primitive or ethnic appearance. Some made of precious metals and gems, some natural and found elements; very little seems to be genuinely ancient.

Artist Jewelry: Mostly handmade, signed, or trademarked by an artist. Includes antique, heirloom, and contemporary items, made of everything from precious metals and stones to plastics.

Beaded: Jewelry of any age, made of small objects, any material, carved, pressed, blown, or molded, with holes pierced all the way through, enabling them to be strung, sewn, or wired.

Carved, Cameo: Any material carved into a small scene, portrait, or vignette used as the focus in a piece of jewelry. Items may be cut, carved, molded (even painted); shell, ivory, lava, stone, mineral, glass, plastics. Category contains antique, heirloom, and contemporary examples, as well as unset cameo carvings.

Charms: Small objects of any material, handmade or manufactured, that contain holes or loops so they may be attached to jewelry. Antique and new examples, including vending-machine plastic charms. Category also contains jewelry made with charms.

Contemporary: Modern jewelry, made from precious gems and metals, as well as plastics, base metals, alloys, rhinestones, and miscellaneous materials. In general, items are brand-new.

Costume

Antique, Vintage: Costume jewelry made before 1900, as well as more recent pieces, are listed here.

Bakelite, Plastics: Contains celluloid, Lucite, acrylics, thermoplastics, as well as Bakelite. Jewelry is carved, molded, laminated, set with rhinestones, painted, or combined with other materials, such as metal or wood.

Designer, Signed: Any jewelry identifiable as the product of a particular designer or manufacturer, displaying a trademark or signature. Unsigned jewelry attributable to specific companies or designers is included.

Contemporary: New or modern costume jewelry, signed or unsigned, made of any "costume" material.

Edwardian: Listings include Edwardian-style items, as well as jewelry actually made during the reign of King Edward VII of England (1901–1910).

Findings: Clasps, jump rings, pinbacks, plaques, stamped motifs, chains, etc.

Fine: Gold and sterling silver, set with gems; antique, vintage, or contemporary.

Gold: Jewelry made of solid gold, 10K, 14K, 18K, antique, heirloom, or contemporary, signed or unsigned.

Gold-Plated: Category contains gold-plated, gold-filled, gold-washed, and gold-tone items.

Novelty: Catchall category, with items made of a variety of materials and unusual motifs, such as fishing, fly jewelry, toe rings, and feather-and-clay Eskimo figures.

Pearls: Category contains listings for pearls, faux pearls, wax beads, and other beads.

Platinum: This category almost exclusively comprises of engagement rings and wedding bands, usually set with diamonds.

Rhinestones: Another catchall category, with listings for anything "fake," whether old or new.

Silver: Any jewelry made of silver, whether plated, coin silver, or sterling. May be old or new, mass-produced or handmade.

General

Antique, Vintage: Some listings are actually for antique pieces; vintage jewelry predominates.

Contemporary: New items and jewelry made during the past decade to complement current fashion trends; may contain any amount of silver.

Designer, Signed: Silver jewelry with trademarks or signatures of the maker, designer, or manufacturer. Items may be antique, vintage, old, used, new, or contemporary, with varying silver content.

Mexican: Reflects a current collecting trend for silver jewelry from Mexico, or Mexican "style." Items may be antique, vintage, used, contemporary, or new, and contain varying amounts of silver.

Silver-Plated: Mostly jewelry items that are not sterling or coin silver, but base metal or copper plated with silver.

Victorian

Mourning: Items made in memory of lost loved ones; materials include onyx, jet, black glass, solid gold, gold plate, rolled gold, silver, brass, vulcanite, seed pearls, human hair, and often include portraits or other mementos of the departed.

Reproduction: Victorian-style items—new, modern, or made anytime since the end of the Victorian era, approximately 1900.

Vintage: Another catchall category, including any jewelry that is not antique, but was made before the present decade. Includes such styles as Art Nouveau, Arts and Crafts, Art Deco, Egyptian Revival, Art Moderne, Post Modern, and other identifiable styles of the past.

Dealing with Dealers

Most dealers are honest. They understand that the key to success is attracting repeat customers. As a beginner, your first task is to find dealers with good reputations, people who have been in the business for years. Select dealers who belong to a trade association with a strong code of ethics, such as the Associated Antiques Dealers of America. A personal recommendation from another collector is a good place to start.

Here are some pointers that will be helpful in your initial encounters with dealers:

- Check out everything in the booth or the shop before you zero in on that one gorgeous piece. This will give you a good idea of the dealer's price range and whether you think her prices are reasonable overall.

- This is a person-to-person business, conducted by humans, so be cheerful and pleasant. If a dealer wants to chat, by all means listen. The best ones have an encyclopedic knowledge of the subject and can be helpful in any number of ways.

- Tell the dealer which piece interests you and ask to see it. At this point she may tell you everything you want to know about the piece. If not, ask questions.

- Examine the jewel, preferably with a loupe. If it is something you want to buy, ask for a discount. A pleasant inquiry, such as "Can you do any better on the price?" or "What is your best price on this?" will usually produce up to a 15% discount. If this puts the item within your price range, you have a deal.

- If the price is still too steep, don't ask for a further discount. Most dealers will get angry if you do this after asking for their best price. And don't disparage the item! A simple "Thanks, but it's a little out of my range" or "It's lovely, but I'll have to think about it" provides a pleasant conclusion.

- Whether or not you make a purchase, tell the dealer that you love her things and ask her to contact you when she acquires a piece similar to what you've admired. Hand her your card, thank her for her time, and leave. You may hear from the dealer when something else comes in. You may hear from her about the particular piece, perhaps at a lower price, after she thinks it over. Or, she may even stop you before you leave the booth or shop. Someone who has been treated with respect will be much more likely to accommodate you, especially when it seems that you may become a regular customer.

Most dealers will tell you everything you want to know about a piece—sometimes more than you want to know. A great dealer knows her specialty. If you still have questions, ask. As with online trading, if the questions are not answered to your satisfaction, move on. The dealer is supposed to help you, to enlarge your body of knowledge, to contribute to your education. Unless dealers can help develop more enthusiasts for their merchandise, they'll have no customers. So you are an important person to the dealer and should be treated as such.

Prices, Prices

Dealers arrive at their prices in varying ways. Remember, this is a business conducted by independent operators. Most got into it, at least in part, because they like to run things their own way.

Some dealers price their wares based solely upon what they paid for each piece. Some base their prices on the current market. Still others just price things based on what they see in other dealers' booths. Most dealers arrive at prices based on a combination of all these factors, and almost all dealers build in a 10% to 25% discount factor. In other words, they anticipate that you'll ask for a discount, so they raise their prices high enough to give you one, while still maintaining their profit.

Occasionally, you'll encounter dealers who don't put prices on their merchandise, preferring to have you ask about each piece. Be wary of this practice. Some experts advise that you not patronize such dealers, who "size up" customers and charge whatever they think the traffic will bear.

If a dealer tells you something about a piece of jewelry and you doubt the information, say thank you politely and move on. When you have a chance to do some research, check out the information. You may find that it was right. Or you may find out that your instincts were correct and the dealer is either misinformed or less than honest. Find another dealer to work with.

If you trusted someone who sold you a fake or reproduction, return the item. Explain politely that you've discovered it isn't real, that there are no hard feelings, but you just can't use it. Most dealers will apologize and offer you a full refund. If you feel that the dealer made an honest mistake and you know that she will stand behind her merchandise, continue shopping with her. (Although you'd be wise to always check her facts in the future.) If you feel that the dealer deliberately gave false information—or she won't refund your money—chalk it up as a cost of your education, and never do business with her again.

Sales Taxes and Receipts

Dealers are required to collect sales tax, with certain exceptions, on every item sold in every U.S. state.

Some dealers use this policy: if you pay by check or by credit card, they will add sales tax to the total since paperwork is gener-

Weiss Cascade
rhinestone
brooch, c. 1950

ated anyway. Some will "forget" the sales tax if you pay in cash. This is illegal. Many dealers don't want to deal in pennies, don't want to calculate the tax, and don't want to make change. The problem is that some don't want to declare the income to the government either, so your cash transaction goes right into their pockets.

No matter how you pay, you are entitled to a receipt for your purchase. However, unless you pay by check or credit card, a dealer may not offer you a receipt, usually because the show is crowded and busy. The dealer should happily furnish you with a receipt if you ask for one, though. Dealers in shops and on the Internet should always give you a receipt. You will be amazed at how many Internet dealers will ship you a package with not even a thank-you note inside, much less a receipt!

A complete sales receipt is the legal contract between a seller and a buyer. It must have the name and address of the dealer. Particularly for a high-ticket item, you want the receipt to include a complete and accurate description of the item, including every single claim the dealer made to you about it. If he says it's Victorian, the receipt should say it is Victorian. If he says it is made of sterling silver, the receipt should say that too. The dimensions, detailed statement of condition, manufacturer, age, and everything else should be on the receipt, along with the store's return policy.

References and Suggested Reading

Design and Creation of Jewelry, 3rd ed., by Robert von Neumann

"Grandma and the Art of Kamikaze Haggling" by Judith Katz-Schwartz, http://www.msjudith.net/other/021199.htm, 1999

Jewelry Concepts and Technology by Oppi Untracht

"Judith's Laws of On-line Auction Commerce: How Not to Get Burned," by Judith Katz-Schwartz, http://www.msjudith.net/other/010199.htm, 1999

Maloney's Antiques and Collectibles Resource Directory, 5th ed., by David Maloney.

TM

NOW THAT YOU'RE READY
TO START COLLECTING

As you begin your search for jewelry, you'll need a few tools to help you make judgments about authenticity, age, dimensions, and condition.

First and foremost, you need a tool to magnify small objects and a light source. One good loupe is the Rubin & Son Triplet 10X 20.5mm Antwerp for magnification. Purchase a good-quality penlight too.

Really look at the object before you use your loupe for close examination. Take note of the design, construction, weight, and the feel. Now take a closer look. Take the loupe in your hand and bring it to your eye. Bring the piece of jewelry up near the loupe. Move the piece back and forth until the field of vision is correct. Keep both eyes open for the best depth of field.

Tools for jewelry collectors

In addition to a loupe and penlight, take along pocket-sized books on marks, a tape measure, a watch/locket opener, plastic jewelry bags and soft wrapping material, and a magnet. The Wyler pocketknife has a special blade for opening pocket watches and lockets (it saves the fingernails). Books on hallmarks, trademarks,

COLLECTOR'S COMPASS

As you examine more and more jewelry, you'll discover that a great deal of information is discernible without using testing solutions. If you've done your homework, you can evaluate a piece of jewelry by visual examination. Examine the item closely; feel it carefully. Then answer these questions:

- Does it have a mark or quality stamp? If so, what does it say? What's the significance?
- Does it have any corners, seams, or raised areas where the color is different, indicating worn plating or surface treatment?
- What color is it?
- How does it feel? Is it heavy and does it lay hard in the palm of your hand?
- Is the piece new?
- Does the surface have a "fake" look—too brassy or too shiny?

maker's marks, and so on, can help you make a great buy or prevent you from making a mistake. A tape measure has many uses, so keep one handy at all times. A magnet—made of iron, steel, or magnetite (lodestone)—can help you instantly separate iron or steel from precious metals. A magnet is a safe test and will not harm jewelry if used with care.

Do not damage someone else's property with any testing procedure (such as scraping or scratching) unless you have express permission. Only the very experienced person should use precious metal testing liquids. When misused, they can be harmful not only to jewelry, but also to people.

What Determines the Value of Jewelry?

Many factors affect the value of jewelry, but the most important of all is "the eye of the beholder." Following are a number of objective criteria, ranked according to impact on value by our experts, starting with the highest. They reflect general marketplace guidelines, but bear in mind that a "defect" may actually be desirable in some collections. Monograms, for instance, usually decrease value since most people don't want to wear someone else's initials. But there are collectors who seek out monogrammed jewelry—for them, its value is increased.

Condition
Just as a realtor will tell you "Location, location, location," a jewelry collector will tell you "Condition is everything."

Collectible jewelry is found for sale in every imaginable state, from pristine to deplorable. The best possible condition is mint. This term gets bandied about in the marketplace, but its meaning is actually very strict. Mint means just exactly as it came from the manufacturer. It means never worn, never touched, never handled, never scratched, and never smudged. As you can imagine, you won't see very many items in mint condition.

A piece of jewelry in excellent condition may have been worn, but it will have no visible flaws. This means no missing, cloudy, scratched, chipped, or dark stones; no missing, worn, or scratched plating or paint; no missing or broken parts; no replacement parts, except stones that have been so expertly replaced that they are indiscernible from the originals, even under magnification.

If you're fortunate, you'll be able to find items in excellent condition to build your collection. Many experts advise that you buy the best you can afford unless it is a piece so rare that you're unlikely ever to see an example of it again. But don't come to that conclusion too readily, especially as a new collector.

Although there is no formal condition rating system for jewelry, some thoughtful and serious collectors have devised useful guidelines for evaluating prospective purchases. Janet Lawwill, proprietor of Sparkles Vintage Costume Jewelry and Fine Estate Jewelry, has posted an excellent set of guidelines at http://www.sparkleplenty.com/info/terms.htm. She carefully ranks the flaws acceptable at each level of condition.

Evaluating Damage

The most common damage to costume jewelry is stones that have fallen out or that have turned dark, cloudy, or black. Since the stones are usually made of glass, damage in the form of chips and cracks is also possible.

With plated metals of all types, the most common damage is worn or missing plating. It is expensive to have a piece replated and

---

The Difference a Little Glue Can Make

One appraiser and authority on antiques recently bought a gorgeous Art Deco costume necklace, bracelet, and earring set. It was of obvious quality, but the stones were tumbling out like leaves. She knew that the glue dries up after fifty years or so.

She purchased the whole set for $25 and plans to remove and reset all the stones, using space-age glue that will last longer than she will. She estimates that the fully restored set will be worth $150.

difficult to get the new plating to look like the old. Worn plating on the back of a piece may be acceptable if the front is outstanding and the damaged plating isn't visible when the jewelry is worn.

Always examine jewelry for broken or missing prongs around the stones, or pieces of metal that have broken off. There may be damaged or missing findings, such as a pin back, or part of the locking clasp on a brooch. The chain on a necklace can break, or the jump ring needed to fasten it can break off. All of these things detract from the desirability—and therefore the value—of a piece of jewelry.

Brooch with worn plating

Fine jewelry made of precious metals and gems is hardier and, with reasonable care, will survive hundreds of years, although delicate links and clasps will often sustain damage. Costume jewelry, on the other hand, is susceptible to harm from just about everything. If the wearer used perfume, lotions, or hairsprays, the plating on the back of her jewelry will most likely be worn or completely gone. If she (good heavens!) perspired, the same thing is likely.

You can easily tell when jewelry has been carelessly stored, exposed to changes in temperature and humidity. Condensation between rhinestones and their foil backing will eventually turn the stones cloudy or black, and this damage is not reversible. Humidity will also encourage the formation of rust or corrosion on the metal. This can be cleaned off, but it will take the plating with it, leaving a black area on the metal. High temperatures can

Scarab bracelet with missing clasp

make stones fall out and cause plating to crack and fall off, as will extremely cold temperatures.

Items stored touching each other may be scratched, dented, or in the case of certain plastics, crumbled into powder. Items left to accumulate dust will exhibit dull stones. Rhinestone jewelry left in the sun will result in cloudy stones. Since some of this damage doesn't show up immediately, it is doubly important to know whom you are dealing with when you buy costume jewelry. A dealer who regularly cleans her costume jewelry in an ultrasonic jewelry cleaner (which is filled with soapy water) will sell you beautiful, shiny jewelry—and all the stones will turn black in a few years, to match the plating that has fallen off, to be replaced by black and green corroded base metal.

Repairs and Restoration

Pass by any piece of jewelry with missing parts, unless the missing part is something you can easily replace or is a part that doesn't show when the item is worn, and the price is so low that the repaired piece will be worth several times the purchase price. A great example of this is a lovely brooch that's missing its pin shaft. That means the entire pin mechanism should be intact, with only the pin stem needing replacement. Stems or shafts may be found at most craft stores and are easily installed with a pair of needle-nose pliers.

Sloppily done repairs, such as amateur resoldering, are not acceptable. When you consider buying a piece, examine it carefully under magnification, stone by stone and inch by inch. Then turn it over and do the same thing. Any globs of solder, metal details that don't match the rest of the piece, stones that are the wrong color or size, or globs of glue are signs that the piece has been repaired—and not very well. Good repairs should be invisible.

If a piece of jewelry has replacement parts, the seller is obligated to relay that information to you. Globs of glue or mismatched stones will devalue any piece. Other repairs, such as soldered parts or new clasps, should be pointed out to the customer, and the piece priced accordingly. Items with missing parts that have been replaced with parts from some other vintage piece are considered "marriages." Some collectors consider these acceptable, some do not, but be a little wary; their value is not as high as

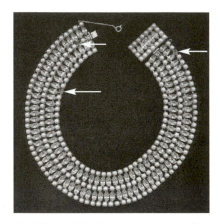

Necklace with three missing pearls

The same necklace with
replacement pearls

Solder
repair

a similar piece with all original parts.

A repair such as resizing a ring, if properly executed, will not adversely affect value. With experience, you can spot repairs like a seam on the shank of a ring, or a replaced finding or fitting. In most cases, if the repair is right for the object and makes it wearable, then negative impact on value is low. If the repair job detracts from the item's beauty or makes it difficult to wear, then the repair is not acceptable and negative impact on value is high.

Repairs and restorations are best left to professionals. A beautifully restored piece can retain 100% of the value of a piece in excellent condition. More than one professional designer started out laboring in another designer's company and can do beautiful restoration work on that designer's jewelry. Any piece of Miriam Haskell jewelry in need of restoration should be sent to Lawrence Vrba, former head designer for the Haskell Company and a successful contemporary designer in his own right. His restoration work is magnificent. (See listings in "Resources to Further Your Collection.")

Wearability and Function

Wearability is important to many jewelry aficionados. If the condition is so poor that they wouldn't be proud to wear it, then its value has been greatly reduced. Occasionally, a piece in poor condition that can be inexpensively restored might be a good investment. This is something you'll learn from experience.

There is also a category of jewelry called mechanicals. Such pieces must be functional for the jewelry to achieve its full potential value. Tremblers must tremble, windmills must turn, and the pendulums on cuckoo-clock charms must swing back and forth. If they don't, a minimum of half the value of the item is lost; in some cases, the piece is worthless.

For specialized collections, value is not impacted by wearability or by functional obsolescence. Although few people actually use sewing chatelaines, silver or gold toothpicks, or train holders (hem lifts), they are avidly sought by collectors.

Original Packaging

A few collectors buy only jewelry in its original packaging. However, it's seldom available, so don't hold your breath.

When original packaging accompanies an object, impact on value is high. In fact, the price could double, depending on the kind of packaging and the category of collectible. If the packaging is in good to mint condition, it is more desirable than if it is in poor or fair condition. A fitted leather box lined with velvet certainly enhances and protects jewelry.

Although original packaging has an impact on value, so does expensive antique-type reproduction packaging. A distributor of this exquisite packaging is Fay Cullen, 2124 N.E. 1223 Street, Suite 209, North Miami, FL 33181; (888) FAYS-BOX or (305) 899-8765 (10 A.M. to 5 P.M. EST). Call her for a brochure. Fay Cullen also sells beautiful Art Deco–style sterling enamel cufflinks and studs. The cufflinks and studs have English hallmarks and can be purchased with a fitted case.

Original fitted packaging

When it comes to costume jewelry, very few pieces ever had original packaging. It was sold through stores and boutiques that supplied their own boxes. Occasionally, you'll come across an original box labeled with the manufacturer's name—it was probably part of a store promotion.

Jewelry of the 1960s and 1970s sometimes came with paper tags and engraved or applied trademarks. The tags add no value since jewelry can't be worn with tags on it; in addition, the tags only trumpet the fact that it's a later piece of jewelry.

Intrinsic Worth

There's a big difference between condition and quality. A beautifully made piece that is well constructed of quality materials will always be desirable, even in less-than-perfect condition. Finely detailed, well-executed jewelry that is creatively designed, well-proportioned, and appropriate for its use is a joy to own and wear, and it commands healthy prices.

Jewelry made by designers and manufacturers known for their attention to quality and demanding standards is enthusiastically sought in the marketplace. Also, jewelry that can be tied in with a particular event or historical period is desirable.

For the novice collector, attributes to look for when making a purchase are good workmanship, soundness of materials used, a well-defined style, and condition.

What one collector considers good design, another might consider bad design. However, if the workmanship is really fine, the piece will

Early Edwardian necklace of citrine quartz, pearl, and gold, in original box, c. 1900 command respect. As for materials, they need not be precious, but they should be respectable for their kind. For example, good specimens of semiprecious gemstones are superior to stones with poor color or cut.

Because there are no timeless standards by which to judge jewelry, the piece exhibiting the most defined style of a given time frame is usually the one most in demand and, therefore, the best piece to buy. Go for a piece whose style is proudly well defined rather than a transition piece whose style is a little bit of this and a little bit of that.

Mosaic jewelry has little or no intrinsic value; its primary value is in its appeal to a collector who assesses its artistry. Evaluate the complexity of design and workmanship, then decide whether the subject matter is appealing. Is it aesthetically pleasing? Is the design complex or simple? Is it complex enough to require a high degree of talent? Is it crafted well? Do you need magnification to verify that the design is made of tiny pieces of glass? Is the face of the mosaic smooth to the touch because the joints are smooth? If the answer is "yes" to all of these questions, then the object is outstanding. Each factor adds to its value.

Antique, heirloom, and collectible jewelry cannot ordinarily be valued according to the weight of its metals or ideal-cut stones because these do not take into account all the other factors that increase or decrease value. However, any piece of jewelry with precious metals or stones, no matter how deplorable its condition, will always retain "scrap" value.

Handmade
Mexican sterling
silver bracelet

Rarity

There are some rare pieces of costume jewelry that almost never appear on the market. One can only guess why they're so rare. Perhaps the design didn't sell well, so the manufacturer discontinued it. Maybe it was too fragile and production had to be halted. Or, as was the case with some designs of the forties, World War II interrupted production when materials became unavailable.

There are limited-edition examples of some jewelry, most of it produced in connection with some event, such as the coronation series produced by Trifari in honor of Queen Elizabeth II of England. No one knows exactly how many were produced, but it is apparent to collectors that these things don't frequently come onto the market. This is particularly true of figural pieces, as they are expensive to produce.

Believe no one about rarity. People love to throw that word around. You are better off observing the market.

Commemorative piece: 1939 New York World's Fair Betty Boop pin

Books on jewelry can give you plenty of historical information that will indicate when something is rare (for example, if a particular jewelry company, such as Staret, was in business for only a few years, its jewelry is going to be comparatively rare). But the recent availability of worldwide information on the Internet has proven many experts wrong. You need to watch and learn for a while. Many auction listings begin with the word "rare." When you see the identical Trifari brooch listed as "rare" three or four times, you'll "know it ain't so, Joe!"

The finest and most unusual pieces will always be rare. Those are the ones that took great talent, time, and work to produce.

Production Anomalies

In some categories of collectibles, production anomalies command high prices, but this is not ordinarily so in jewelry. Collectors want jewelry to be as nearly perfect as possible, so design flaws, mistakes, or glitches are not valued.

Variations

Variations, which are usually intended by the maker, are collectible, as most collectors strive to complete a set of variants. The Trifari poppy set was made in more than one color. The less common colors are immediately snapped up by collectors.

Attribution

There is no doubt that certain designers' work commands higher prices than others. This tends to change based on changing fashions, discoveries in the marketplace about rarity, an article or publication of a new book that brings heightened attention to a designer or manufacturer, and just plain fickleness.

At the end of the 1990s, anything by Eisenberg commanded astronomical prices, mostly because it was thought to be difficult

---

What's in a Name?

Some designers of highly sought-after jewelry are immediately recognized by only one name:

Fabergé: A Russian designer, goldsmith, and jeweler whose work was lavish. He created masterpieces for Czar Nicholas. In addition to quality marks, Fabergé used a designer mark in the form of a signature. He also employed work masters who had marks of their own.

Hobé: A twentieth-century American costume jewelry designer and manufacturer. Founded in 1903, the company is still in business.

Lalique: One of the foremost designers of the Art Nouveau period. He used a signature as a designer mark.

Monet: A twentieth-century American costume jewelry manufacturer/designer from 1937.

Spratling: Trained as a designer, William Spratling settled in Taxco, Mexico, in 1929, where he started a shop to make and sell jewelry. One of the "hottest" collectibles has been Mexican designer jewelry. Spratling used a stylized signature of his initials as a designer mark.

Unger Bros.: A company of silversmiths and jewelers who mass-produced jewelry and received patents for Art Nouveau designs. Unger's mark is a superimposed UB trademark.

---

to find. Once it became apparent that Eisenberg was plentiful on eBay and that, although very well made, the majority of pieces with clear stones were both boring and deteriorating rapidly, prices for Eisenberg jewelry fell. A year later, only the very best pieces, those with colored stones, still sold for high prices.

The best work of a favored designer is always desirable. Every piece of jewelry should be turned over and scanned with a loupe to see if it is signed. Often it is possible to recognize a particular company or designer's work by the style, construction, and materials of the piece. Nonetheless, a signed piece will always command a higher price, partly because people are afraid to trust their own judgment or that of the dealer. They want to see an impressed trademark on the back of the piece. This is unfortunate in the case of a company like Schreiner, which made only the highest-quality pieces but left many of them unsigned. The use of certain materials, such as odd-shaped colored stones and unique hook-and-eye construction, makes Schreiner's work unmistakable, but if it's unsigned, it's worth only about 75 percent of the value of a signed piece.

Some of the most collectible signatures in costume jewelry are Trifari, Miriam Haskell, Schreiner New York, Weiss, Kramer New York, Hollycraft, Coro, Corocraft, Chanel, De-Mario, Stanley Hagler, Mazer, Jomaz, Regency, Original by Robert, and Boucher. If you're intent on building a serious collection of costume jewelry, it's a good idea to spend the time to familiarize yourself with these names and research their various designs. While the names are highly recognized and esteemed, some of the designs of each are much more valuable than others. The names alone do not command premium prices.

Schreiner rhinestone brooch

Provenance

Provenance does factor into desirability and, thus, value. Most of the jewelry-collecting world was astounded when Gloria Vanderbilt put some of her own collection up on eBay and it realized prices far beyond the intrinsic value of the jewelry. There was nothing terribly rare or luxurious in the offerings.

Jewelry owned by a celebrity, if it has proof of provenance, will often command outrageous prices. In this territory, you are in direct competition with devotees who collect that celebrity's memorabilia. This is not an area of jewelry collecting for the faint of heart or the light of pocket.

As with any collectible, if there is concrete provenance for a piece of jewelry, its value rises. But it must be established and demonstrated as a fact; hearsay does not establish authenticity. If, for instance, a piece of jewelry allegedly owned and worn by a famous historical figure is accompanied by a photograph or painting of her wearing it, expect it to be a very costly piece.

Jackie's Jewels

Does provenance add value? You bet it does, when the jewels in question were worn by Jacqueline Kennedy Onassis. Here are just a few of the results from Sotheby's 1996 auction:

DESCRIPTION	PRESALE ESTIMATE	SALE PRICE
Two simulated pearl necklaces; two simulated diamond and pearl ear clips	$250–$350	$112,500
Gilt metal cuff bracelet by Kenneth Jay Lane and bangle bracelet	150–200	13,800
Four tribal style necklaces, one stamped "Made in Kenya"	350–450	20,700
Simulated turquoise, emerald, and diamond necklace	100–150	48,875
Bedouin jewelry	400–600	6,900
Black stone bead double-strand necklace, worn by Jackie when JFK announced his candidacy for president	200–300	101,500
Silver and niello belt	500–700	8,625

From time to time, "important" collections go up for sale and prices are crazy, as in the recent auction of some of Barbra Streisand's jewelry. There was nothing in the group that was even close to outstanding, and yet the prices earned were quite high. Again, the publicity machine at the auction house and Streisand's avid memorabilia fans drove the bidding; it had little to do with the factors that ordinarily affect the value of jewelry.

If you're going to buy a piece based on the fame of its previous owner, you should expect written documentation, signed by the seller and at least one previous owner. It should also be in writing that, if the provenance is ever proved false, the item will be returned for a complete refund. The provenance should include a thorough and detailed description of the item, the name of the maker, and the place and date of its manufacture.

Age

Older pieces are not necessarily more valuable than newer ones to jewelry collectors. If an item was poorly designed, unattractive, or inappropriate 100 years ago, it is likely still undesirable today. Age does not increase its value.

Many collectors concentrate on a single era, such as the 1860s or the 1940s, where age defines the collection. While others concentrate on individual designers—such as Miriam Haskell, for example—her earliest pieces were not the best ones. The age of a piece is usually only significant in that it adds to your body of knowledge about the piece and its maker. It is important to collectors to be able to establish an approximate date for each piece in a collection, and there are a number of ways you can do this.

Hallmarks, Maker's Marks, Trademarks

Hallmarks are official marks, first adopted in England in 1300 by Edward I. Hallmarks can be stamped, incised, or punched on gold or silver to show quality and to signify purity of metal according to the sterling or karat standard.

Other marks used on old jewelry can include:

- Commemorative—used during the period of some special event
- Design registration—a kite-shaped registry mark on British-made pieces; indicates registration date but not the date of manufacture
- Duty mark—formerly used to show payment of import duty
- Foreign goods mark—to show date of importation

Trademarks, maker's marks, and designer marks are very important in identifying jewelry. All three can help to date an object and verify origin, manufacturer, wholesaler, or retailer.

Since almost all makers of costume jewelry in the modern era have redesigned their logos and

Wedgwood trademark

trademarks at some time, the design of the trademark is helpful in dating fashion jewelry. For instance, Hollycraft included the year of manufacture as part of its logo during the 1950s, which enables exact dating.

Patent Year

Patent numbers are issued sequentially in the chronological order in which they're granted, with separate sequences for mechanical invention and design patents. Knowing the patent number allows positive dating of when an item was first made with patent protection. However, makers often used "patent pending" marks during the lengthy application process, so a piece may have been produced prior to the patent being granted.

It's also important to remember that the patent number dates to the first year of an item's patent protection. A design or mechanical component could stay in production for many years and would still carry the same patent number. Design patents are granted for fourteen years, invention patents for seventeen.

As they pertain to jewelry, mechanical (invention) patents are granted for unique functional innovations, such as a clasp, a clip, or the like. Design patents are granted for the components and configuration of the aesthetic design itself. Mechanical patents for the twentieth-century are all in the seven-digit range. Design patents began to appear on jewelry around the early 1930s, when the sequence was up to five digits; it reached six digits in 1936. Patented designs may be marked "Des. Pat." or "D" plus the number. The number may also appear by itself. There's no official position for patent markings on jewelry pieces. Makers put them wherever they would fit. So you often have to use your loupe diligently to discover these numbers.

Patent-date lists for both mechanical (invention) patents and design patents are widely available and are even published on a set of laminated cards by *Antiques and Collectibles Reproduction News*. The U.S. Patent and Trademark Office has a web site, www.uspto.gov, where you can find further info on design patents and a link to a list of issue years and patent numbers.

Publications

Most twentieth-century jewelry makers didn't publish catalogs as we know them. Instead they sent salesmen out with samples of their wares. They did, however, advertise in all the women's magazines, so old copies of *Vogue* and *Glamour* can be great sources of information to help date jewelry.

Look at Deana Farneti Cera's excellent book *Amazing Gems* for highly reliable dating information. The same is true of *Jewels of Fantasy*, also by Farneti Cera.

Technology and Materials

Understanding how and when various types of findings and fittings evolved can be helpful in determining a "circa" date. Findings (small metal components used to make or repair jewelry, either handmade or mass-produced) not only help date jewelry, but also provide clues about additions, repairs, or alterations. These elements are known as fittings in the British market.

When supplies of rhodium and alloys used in the making of white metal became scarce during World War II, companies began to turn out sterling silver jewelry. Trifari, under the design leadership of Alfred Phillipe, went a step further. The company began using Lucite, the name Du Pont trademarked in 1937 for its version of the acrylic plastic and also known by the trade name Plexiglas, in combination with sterling silver to make its wonderful figural "jelly bellies."

Classic Eisenberg brooch, reissued in 1998

Decorations can also help you date a piece of jewelry. For example, the cut of a stone often determines age: rose-cut stones were popular during the Georgian and early Victorian eras. They became popular again toward the end of the nineteenth century.

There are two excellent sources for learning about techniques of construction and fabrication. The first is *Jewelry Concepts and Technology* by Oppi Untracht. The second is to spend time with a jewelry repair specialist—a great way to learn jewelry construction and gain firsthand knowledge about jewelry in need of repair or restoration.

The Trained Eye

Educate your eyes as well as your brain. A trained eye will be able to date old jewelry. Differences in scale, proportion, and visual nuances become conspicuous to the trained eye that's carefully examined hundreds, preferably thousands, of pieces of jewelry.

Training does not happen overnight. It starts by taking advantage of every opportunity to see and handle authentic pieces of old jewelry and storing up these impressions. Start a memory bank. Visit every museum or exhibition that includes old jewelry. Look at every piece. Note workmanship, techniques, design execution, and artistic merit. Store these images in your mind or write them in a notebook for future reference.

Visit antiques shows where only antique and collectible pieces (not reproductions) are allowed. Ask if you can hold the pieces. Visit an antique jewelry auction. Auctions usually provide a preview time for hands-on inspection. Compare these impressions with your impressions of new reproduction lines of old jewelry. In other words, familiarize yourself with both old and new jewelry before you attempt to determine age.

How to Tell the Real Thing from a Reproduction, Fake, Fantasy, or Revival

It seems that whenever a collectible of any kind gains enough recognition to command high prices, someone will find a way to reproduce it. The creator of a knockoff may be selling her designs with a tag that says they're copies, but unscrupulous dealers soon remove the tags and try to palm off the new pieces as old ones. It takes an alert and sharp eye to catch this. In some instances, there are so many fakes that there's great argument over which is the real version. The result is that the market for the item, including the original version, is killed when consumers stop buying because they're afraid they'll get burned.

There are some well-known fakers of costume jewelry and some well-known fakes. The Trifari stork brooch is an excellent example. There are at least six variations, and no one is quite sure which is the original—including at least one author who published a photo in a book of a "real" one that cannot possibly be authentic. So how do you keep from mistaking a reproduction for an old piece?

First, remember this: If it seems too good to be true, it probably is. If you're offered a rare piece for a song, especially by a dealer unknown to you whose booth contains many extremely rare pieces, back away slowly and run for the door.

Know your subject. Reread "The Trained Eye" in the previous

section. If you're hoping to own a Corocraft Fighting Fish some-day, learn what it looks like. Learn that the fins at the top are sup-posed to be closed and that the enameling extends all the way to the end of the fins. Learn the colors of the eyes and what the back is supposed to look like. Learn what the trademark looks like and where it should be placed. This is another piece that's become the subject of fakes. (For a look at the real thing, turn to page 64.)

There are also dealers selling fake acrylic "Bakelite." It won't pass any of the Bakelite tests (run it under hot water and sniff—Bakelite will smell like formaldehyde, and this won't; it won't make that distinctive clunking sound when two pieces are tapped togeth-er). So if you know that black, heavily carved Bakelite bangles are selling for $300, and someone offers you one for $100, don't reck-lessly jump at an apparent steal. Education is your best defense. And always, always get a proper receipt for each purchase. You should be able to return any fake piece for a refund.

There is certainly a legitimate place in the market for repro-ductions of any antique or collectible. There's just no place for unmarked reproductions. The combination of a thorough educa-tion, a sharp eye, and a receipt should go far to protect you.

In contrast to unauthorized reproductions, fantasy items, and fakes, manufacturers' reissues of old pieces can be a wonderful thing to collect. Dealers who carry the original production pieces may not agree, because the *restrikes* (which use the original molds and materials) will likely result in decreased demand for the earli-er pieces they're selling. But for the collector, reissues can be great. You get an exact duplicate of the old piece. It's made of the same materials with the same molds, and it's in perfect condition. Most manufacturers who reissue designs clearly mark jewelry to distin-guish it from the old pieces. Eisenberg marks its reissues "Eisenberg Ice." Trifari dates the new pieces. They are all quite handsome.

To help you spot known fakes, some of your fellow collectors have put up Web pages that show the differences between the authentic and fake pieces. You'll find a great one for costume jewelry by Rhinestone Rainbow's Deborah Kosnett located at www.marketplace.com.

If you are still in doubt about the identity or authenticity of a piece of costume jewelry, get an expert opinion. If you've joined Jewelcollect, you can post a picture of the item on the Web and query the group as to the identification of your find. Once you know what you have, you can search for it on eBay and see recent selling prices of similar pieces.

If it's a really expensive item and you want to be certain it's genuine, you can pay an expert to thoroughly research and evaluate the piece for you. Try to get a recommendation for a certified appraiser in your area from another jewelry collector. If you're an Internet user, two of the national appraisal organizations—International Society of Appraisers (ISA) and American Society of Appraisers (ASA)—have Web sites that feature state-by-state member directories. If you have to resort to the yellow pages, look for appraisers who are certified by one of these organizations. When you call, ask if they're jewelry specialists.

Several entities are in the process of setting up Web sites where you can have an item evaluated. The average cost is about $20 per item.

Doing your own research begins to sound better and better, right?

Building Your Collection

There are a number of conventional ways to go about building a collection, and at least hundreds of unconventional ways. Some of the more traditional—by designer, manufacturer, material, motif, like items, series—were reviewed in "Jewelry as a Collectible." By now, you probably have a pretty good idea of what you want the thrust of your collecting to be.

As a newcomer to the hobby, you'll probably want to steer clear of trendy, "hot" items, because you'll find yourself paying top dollar until you can build your skills and establish a network in the marketplace. Otherwise, anything goes! Collect what appeals to you, what pleases you, what gives you joy.

Some types of costume jewelry are receiving little or no attention from collectors. A beginner could acquire great numbers of these items at really low prices. Wooden figurals are very inexpensive now, as are well-made pieces by lesser-known companies such as Lisner or Art.

Once you've learned your way around the market and assembled a nice collection, you're sure to want to "trade up," to acquire some pieces that reflect your changing tastes as you become more sophisticated. If your funds are limited (and whose aren't?), it's best to concentrate on one thing.

The "Business" of Collecting

Be sure to keep accurate records and current insurance information on your collection. Protecting your jewelry in this way will pay dividends many times over, and unless you amass a huge and extremely valuable collection, these chores won't take much of your time.

Maintaining Good Records

Save your receipts. One good idea is to staple the dealer's business card to the receipt. For online purchases, save all e-mail between you and the seller. It is difficult to get a receipt from many businesses on the Web, so it's doubly important to save credit card bills, e-mail, and any other documents pertaining to the sale.

If you are well organized, keeping track of sellers with whom you deal is helpful for many reasons:

- You can contact the dealer if there is a problem with the merchandise you purchased.
- You can inquire whether the dealer has any other similar pieces for you.
- You may want to do business with the dealer, perhaps to sell back something in order to buy a better piece.
- You can supply the dealer with your "want list." It's a good idea to have copies to give out to dealers at shows. Keep the list updated—don't squander valuable dealer contacts by having them watch out for pieces you acquired long ago.
- You may need to refer to the receipt if you can't remember what you paid for the item or you need to document its value. This is useful if you want to insure it or resell it.
- You may want to refer to the records of your dealings with a particular seller to establish what kind of discount to expect.
- You may want to ask this dealer to appraise something for you.
- If you've had a good experience with a dealer, you may want to recommend her to other collectors, especially beginners.

Making an Inventory

Keeping an inventory should be simple. There are a number of software programs available for inventory management if you want to use your computer. There is a free one at www.collector online.com.

If you prefer to keep handwritten records, photocopy the "Welcome to My Collection" form provided on page 94. (You may make as many copies as you need for personal use, but it is a violation of copyright to sell or distribute them to others.) Complete a form for each new addition to your collection.

Photographic records of your jewelry are a great idea. Forget video; if you are close enough to see any detail, the jewelry will be out of focus. You're much better off using a scanner for jewelry. It takes the best pictures. If you don't have a computer and a scanner, a 35mm single-lens reflex camera with a macro lens will do the job.

Lighting jewelry properly for photography is difficult. Make sure you have a tripod, a neutral background (medium gray works best for most jewelry), and white fabric (ripstop nylon works best) or tissue paper to put over the lights. Otherwise, the reflections off stones will ruin every picture. You can record all the pertinent information on the back of each photo, and there's your inventory system!

Storage is of paramount importance. You need a cool, dry place, where the temperature and humidity don't vary. Long-term storage in plastic bags is not advisable! The best arrangement is to get jewelers' trays and line them with velvet pads or sheets of upholstery foam. The trays stack and you can fit a lot of jewelry in them, but be sure none of it is touching any other pieces. Before you stack the next tray atop the one you just filled, throw in a little packet of desiccant silica gel (the packets come in your vitamin bottle or are packed with camera lenses).

Never store celluloid in a closed container with other plastics. The celluloid can get "celluloid sickness," which causes it to crumble and then give the disease to your other plastics.

WELCOME TO MY COLLECTION

Date of purchase:_____

Purchase price:_____

Description (what it is, dimensions, visual appearance):

_____

_____

_____

_____

Construction materials (metals or stones used):_____

_____

Embellishments (engraving, intaglio): _____

Condition (e.g., excellent, worn, needs repair):_____

_____

Age (how and by whom it was determined):_____

Comments (e.g., limited edition, provenance):_____

_____

_____

_____

_____

From whom purchased: _____

Address:_____

_____

_____

Telephone/fax:_____

E-mail:_____

Getting an Appraisal

An official appraisal is a thoroughly researched, written, and certified evaluation of an item or collection. It must include the reason for the appraisal (different reasons will result in different values); a complete description of the items, including photos; the research method used; the resources consulted; the valuation method used; and the market for which it is being evaluated.

Few collectors would invest in an appraisal just to satisfy their curiosity or ascertain whether their jewels are appreciating satisfactorily. However, an appraisal may be warranted if you want to

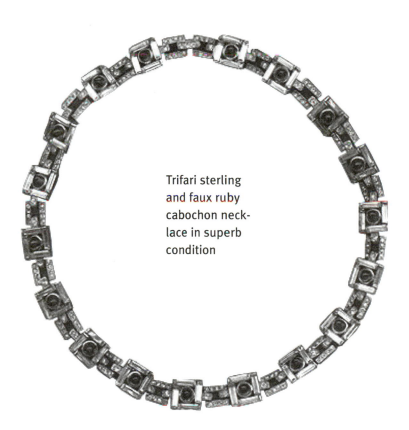

Trifari sterling and faux ruby cabochon necklace in superb condition

insure a collection, sell it, or donate it to a charity for the tax write-off. It could also be useful in establishing its value as part of a divorce settlement or other lawsuit, or for dividing your collection among your heirs in planning your estate. In short, you need to have a purpose for getting an appraisal, and the appraiser must know what it is.

The best way to locate a qualified appraiser is by referral. Your attorney will be able to recommend someone he has used. The local auction house probably has someone to whom they can refer

Unsigned multicolored
rhinestone necklace

you. Or one of the appraisal societies can recommend a local member. If you want to search online, try the International Appraisal Society's web site at http://isa-appraisers.org.

You want someone who specializes in antique and collectible jewelry. An appraiser of fine jewelry should also be a gemologist (or should work in collaboration with one). Ask to see the appraiser's credentials. If he refuses, move on. Do not hire any appraiser whose fee is a percentage of the value of your collection. An honest and ethical appraiser will never charge that way. Also, never hire anyone who tells you he wants first crack at your collection if you sell. It is absolutely unethical for an appraiser to evaluate anything in which he has an interest, or to offer to buy anything he has appraised. Expect to be quoted either an hourly or flat-rate fee.

Remember that an appraisal document is admissible as evidence in a court of law. Everything in that document should be laid out clearly, including any experts the appraiser may have consulted during its preparation. It is also a confidential document. Appraisers are bound by the same client-professional privilege as attorneys and doctors, so they cannot give out any information about you or your collection. Copies of the appraisal may be forwarded to other people only upon your written request.

Expect the appraiser to require you to sign a contract. The contract should be specific, with the date of completion of the report spelled out and a detailed description of the service to be provided. The fee should be included in the contract, as well as a payment schedule (usually 50% upon signing the contract, with the balance to be paid upon delivery of the report).

Remember that the appraiser must spend long hours doing research and writing your report, and he will expect to be paid for his time. It's possible that the resulting fee may be higher than the value of your collection, and an ethical appraiser will tell you beforehand whether it makes sense to hire him. Only you can judge whether it is worthwhile to proceed.

Insuring a Collection

Depending on the size and value of your collection, you may want to insure it. You can attach a rider to your homeowner's policy, but this is usually expensive and may be restricted to fine jewelry—items valued in the thousands of dollars. Consult your agent, because many insurance companies consider jewelry to be "ordinary household contents" unless exceptional pieces are document-ed and listed individually. The premium will be high, and insur-ance will not reimburse you for more than intrinsic value (the item's value as a collectible will be lost).

There are companies that specialize in collectibles insurance, and several authorities recommend these low-cost policies as the best choice. Look for their ads in trade journals. Also, you'll find that some collector's clubs and associations offer group rates—another benefit of joining.

References and Suggested Reading

Antiques and Collectibles Reproduction News, patent-date cards:
   (800) 227-5531 or www.repronews.com
Amazing Gems by Deana Farneti Cera
American Jewelry Manufacturers by Dorothy T. Rainwater
Art Deco Fashion and Jewelry by Rebecca Kingsley
Collecting Rhinestone and Colored Jewelry, 3rd ed., by Maryanne
   Dolan
Is It Real or Fake? by Deborah Kosnett
   www.rhinestonerainbow.com/realfake.htm/
Jewelry Concepts and Technology by Oppi Untracht
Jewels of Fantasy by Deana Farneti Cera
Sparkles Vintage Costume Jewelry Condition Guide by Janet Lawwill,
   http://www.sparkleplenty.com/info/terms.htm

LIVING WITH YOUR JEWELRY COLLECTION

Lucky you! Not only do you have the enormous pleasure of amassing your jewelry collection, but—unlike the majority of collectors—you get to share it with friends, colleagues, and strangers every day. Can you imagine an accountant showing up to a business meeting with a few specimens from his tin toy collection? Or a collector navigating the grocery store aisles with some Depression glass in tow?

One collector finds words inadequate to describe the pleasure she derives from her jewelry. She is always adorned with something. Even when wearing jeans or sweats, she adds a pin or bracelet. She collects both elegant jewelry and plastic brooches and figurals that lend themselves to casual clothing and relaxed occasions.

Another jewelry collector, who also lectures widely on her hobby, says her collection has changed her self-image. She used to marvel at how "pulled together" some women looked. Now she realizes that she controls her "look" by the way she accessorizes. "I can take one dress and make it look casual, businesslike, dressy, or formal, simply by changing jewelry. My wardrobe has many black outfits, because black is the best background for my jewelry!"

A collector with her treasures

New Uses for Old Jewels

Some collectors have a lot of fun experimenting. One decided to see how many ways she could discover to wear her dress clips. Since clips have a limited intended use (to be worn at the corners of a sweetheart neckline), they posed a particular challenge.

She has worn them on belts, on shoes, on hats, on collars, on a coat, on her watchband, on a handbag, and even on the hem of a shirt or sleeve to admiring glances!

Displaying Your Collection

Many jewelry collectors choose not to display their collections in the conventional sense. The jewelry is on display when the collectors wear it, and pieces left behind are protected from light, humidity, and dust in a closed case.

However, there certainly are many collectors who do want to be surrounded by their objets d'art. One collector pins her brooches to wide swaths of ribbon hanging on the walls. Another has a big glass-and-oak curio cabinet, in which her jewels are displayed on velvet pads, as if they were in a museum.

Many collectors create "pictures," having a singular example or a whole grouping mounted, matted, and framed. Deep frames or shadowboxes also work well and can be mounted on the wall or displayed on tables or shelves. You can buy shadowboxes that are meant to be sealed, or the type with hinges so items can be removed or rearranged easily.

There are several types of glass-topped display tables made specifically for small objects like jewelry. You'll find them advertised in trade papers.

If you are going to display your collection, you may want to light it. Ordinary incandescent or fluorescent lighting—of the type used to illuminate paintings—won't harm most jewelry. But there is an important exception: certain gemstones, such as morganite, will fade when exposed to strong, prolonged light. Check with a gemologist about safe lighting for natural gemstones because, when the body color is altered, so is the value. All jewelry should be kept out of direct sunlight and away from heat.

Caring for Your Collection

Storage and Protection

When you're not wearing it, keep jewelry protected from humidity, extremes of temperature, sunlight, dust, grease, and contact with other pieces of jewelry. Jewelry trays lined with velvet pads are available from jewelry supply houses. The trays stack nicely and you can fit quite a lot into a reasonable amount of space in a closet or drawer.

One collector had some dresser drawers lined with velvet. Her jewelry is stored in the dresser, and she can choose what she wants at a glance.

A printer's cabinet is an ideal storage space because the drawers are shallow and there are dividers in each one. Just be sure the interior is perfectly clean and lined with something that won't scratch your jewelry.

If you live in a humid environment, you can purchase cotton bags of moisture-absorbing clay and hang them in the cabinet or closet. When they're saturated, they can be dried out in the oven and reused. A dish of cat litter in a closed cabinet where you are storing jewelry will also absorb moisture. Never take your jewelry off and leave it in the bathroom, not even temporarily.

Avoid keeping your jewelry in rooms with no heat or air conditioning. Extreme temperatures or swings in temperature can cause opals or glass embellishments to crack or craze. Use the Ultra Filter Shield to combat airborne dust and mold (it is also antimicrobial). Order filters from Scan Air Filter Company, 100 Beta Drive, Franklin, TN 37064, (615)790-2019.

COLLECTOR'S COMPASS™

If you insure your collection, the carrier may have strict rules concerning how it can be displayed. Check with your insurance agent about the type of security required.

Don't store jewelry in plastic bags for any length of time. It needs air circulation. Use acid-free tissue paper instead. To store pieces you won't wear for a while, put them in individual cardboard boxes. Use the kind you get when you buy jewelry in a

COLLECTOR'S COMPASS

Never, ever clean your costume jewelry in an ultrasonic jewelry cleaner or any other device that requires you to use water. Even if it isn't ruined immediately, the stones will turn black and the metal will corrode in a matter of days, weeks, or even years.

Used carefully, according to manufacturer's instructions, ultrasonic cleaners are usually safe for fine jewelry. However, some gemstones—specifically opals and turquoise—should never be put in an ultrasonic cleaner. Neither should pearls—natural or cultured. Other than these exceptions, just make sure that the jewelry you're going to clean is made exclusively of gemstones and solid metal (gold, silver, platinum, or palladium) with absolutely no plating or foil-backed stones.

department store or boutique, with the cotton inserts, and stack them.

Care and Cleaning

Try not to handle your jewelry after putting on perfume or lotion, or when your hands are oily or sticky. Actually, white cotton gloves are the ideal thing to wear when handling jewelry, but who wants to put them on every time you pick up an item?

Pearls are especially sensitive to hairsprays and skin oils, which alter their color and luster. Put on pearl jewelry when you are ready to go. Store pearls in original packaging or a soft cloth bag. Protect their beauty by wiping them with a clean, soft cloth before putting them away.

Costume jewelry will require only an occasional dusting with a soft brush, such as the kind used to put on blusher. Never use water on metal or stones. Real dirt and grime should be removed with rubbing alcohol, applied with a cotton swab. The stones can be cleaned, carefully, with ammoniated window cleaner, also using a cotton swab. Be sure none of the cleaner runs down into the setting. If the foil backing gets wet, it will eventually turn the stone black. The cleaner can also corrode base metals over time.

Warm soapy water is fine for cleaning plastic jewelry without stones, followed by a wipe with a soft cloth. Bakelite may be cleaned with Simichrome polish, available from jewelry supply houses. Sunshine cloths, also sold by jewelry supply houses and some antiques stores, are wonderful for polishing jewelry and bringing up a nice shine.

Do not use Simichrome or any other metal polish on plated jewelry; it will remove the plating. Ketchup will take green corrosion off base metals. Just leave it on for a few minutes, then wipe off and clean with alcohol on a cotton swab. Be aware that, in place of the green stuff, you may find a black spot. Corrosion is oxidation, so the metal has combined with oxygen to form a new compound. When you remove it, you're taking off what once was the plating.

Repairs and Restoration

With a little practice, you can reset missing stones yourself. Janet Lawwill of Sparkles Vintage Jewelry has posted a useful set of guidelines at her Web site, www.sparkleplenty.com/info/clean.htm.

It's also a simple matter to replace a broken jump ring from a necklace or bracelet, or a pin shaft. Supplies and tools for these repairs may be found at your local craft store, or try B'Sue's supply page at www.bsue.com/adornment/supplies.htm or FDJ Tools at www.fdj-tool.com.

COLLECTOR'S COMPASS™

Carefully read—and heed—manufacturer's instructions on any cleaning or polishing compound. Pearls, hair, plastic, shell, and amber, among other jewelry components, can be easily damaged or destroyed. When in doubt, don't use it.

Use properly matched parts: stones of the same color, shape, size, and quality; jump rings that exactly match the style and color of the original. If you make simple repairs carefully, they should not affect the value of the item at all. If you should sell it, you are obligated to reveal any repairs to the prospective buyer. So practice on the low-end pieces and, when you get good at it, move on to the better ones.

Unless you're an experienced craftsman with the proper tools, don't try repainting enamel, soldering broken pieces, or replating. Never try to make repairs that strengthen or replace functional parts. Your repair could damage the piece beyond the help of a professional.

If you're determined to tackle complex repairs, consult *Jewelry Concepts and Technology* by Oppi Untracht, or take a course from a local jewelry workshop or community college.

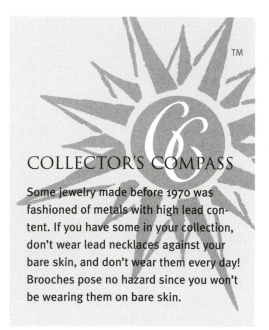

COLLECTOR'S COMPASS

Some jewelry made before 1970 was fashioned of metals with high lead content. If you have some in your collection, don't wear lead necklaces against your bare skin, and don't wear them every day! Brooches pose no hazard since you won't be wearing them on bare skin.

The best way to find a qualified repair person is by referral. Ask members of your jewelry club or other collectors. Ask to see some of the person's previous work. A good restoration can work magic. Jewelry can be replated, re-enameled, restoned, rebeaded, or restrung "as good as new." On the other hand, resoldering is the most difficult repair job to disguise and will probably reduce the value somewhat.

Repairs done professionally and with regard for the integrity of the piece may enhance value; poorly done they will surely detract. For instance, if a ring is resized using solder that matches its content of sterling silver, gold, or platinum, as the case may be, the value is undiminished. Lead solder used in repairs of fine jewelry will invariably reduce its value. Obviously, repairs should not alter or obliterate any part of the piece's original design.

If an item of jewelry is in poor condition, but it is the work of a top-notch designer, it is worthwhile to restore it. Its value may increase substantially, but it will be expensive to do it properly.

Sometimes a piece has minor monetary value, but has great sentimental value to you. The cost of the repair may be more than the piece is worth, but you'll feel it was a good investment when it comes home looking spectacular. And no repair that makes a poor piece look better will ever diminish its value.

References and Suggested Reading

Costume Jewelers: The Golden Age of Design by Joanne Dubbs Ball
Hidden Treasures: Rhinestone Jewelry from Venture Entertainment Group (video series)
Sparkles Cleaning and Repair Tips by Janet Lawwill

*I*F AND WHEN YOU DECIDE TO SELL

Difficult as it may be to believe now, there are many possible reasons you might want to sell part or all of your collection someday. The most common is to "trade up." Your taste has changed, and you've found a new romance with, say, Art Nouveau. Out with the old, in with the new!

Or perhaps you bought the best quality and condition you could afford when you started out, and now you can afford better. It's amazing what you consider acceptable until you go to a convention or high-end show and see examples in pristine condition. As you become more knowledgeable, you're more likely to want only superb examples. So you're ready to sell the old to finance the upgrade.

Also, there is a range from mediocre to fabulous pieces in every designer's repertoire. If you bought a lot of the less inspired work in the beginning, now you may want to acquire the best pieces. Many collectors find that they can trade duplicates or ordinary pieces to secure a "crown jewel" for their collections—another reason it's important to network with others and join a collecting group.

Unsigned rhinestone brooch

Sometimes people find that they need cash more than they need the collection. Or a buyer comes along and makes an offer too good to refuse. And some collectors donate their jewels to a museum, historical society, or other institution to prevent relatives (who rarely appreciate the value of a good collection) from breaking it up or giving it to the local thrift shop.

Selling a Whole Collection

Selling to a Dealer or Buyer

If you want to sell your collection quickly and be done with it, selling it to a dealer or another collector will save you time. It won't necessarily be easy to find a collector willing to take your entire inventory unless you've got some really outstanding items, but you'll net a higher overall price by selling to someone willing to pay closer to retail than pure wholesale.

On the other hand, any dealer who buys your whole collection will expect you to discount substantially to wholesale. She has to cover her overhead and build her own profit into the deal, or she won't buy. Expect to make far less than you will if you do all the work of selling it piece by piece to fellow collectors. And expect that some dealers will attempt to "cherry pick," for the best jewelry and leave you with the rest.

Consignment

Consigning your collection to a jewelry dealer or a resale shop requires minimal effort, but it may take a long time to sell. Because you're taking up substantial space in the booth or shop, you and the dealer will have to agree on selling prices. As each piece is sold, the dealer extracts a commission and pays you the difference. Bear in mind that few dealers will work hard to sell your collection this way; they'll make more money on their own merchandise.

Becoming Your Own Dealer

In order to reap a profit, many collectors opt to become dealers. Indeed, one authority says, "I believe collectors never stop collecting. They become dealers to support their habit!"

There are several ways to sell your collection yourself, one piece at a time. You'll need to use a combination of two or more if you anticipate selling it in a reasonable time.

And remember, once you become a dealer—even if it's only for the short-term disposition of your own collection—you must be prepared to clean, price, and present the merchandise with detailed descriptions. And you should consult your accountant or tax preparer about your obligations to collect and pay state sales tax and income tax on your gain realized by selling.

Shows

This can be one of the hardest—and most rewarding—venues for a new dealer. Be prepared for physical labor, long hours, and the possibility of substantial expense. From your collecting days on the other side of the counter, you'll have an idea which shows in your geographical locale attract jewelry collectors. If you go further afield to the big regional and national shows (see the listings in "Resources to Further Your Collection"), you may face stiff competition just to get a space.

Show dealers generally have to buy equipment, such as showcases, tables and tablecloths, a van, signs, business cards, and receipts. Then there's booth rent and hotel, food, and travel costs. Dealers must clean and tag the merchandise, pack, drive to the city where the show is held, unload the van, and set up a complete store. They have to occupy the booth constantly for several days, haggle endlessly, watch for shoplifters, and comply with show rules—sometimes from 5 A.M. "early buying" until 5 P.M. or later. Then it's time to break down the store, repack, load the van, drive home, and unpack it all again.

Mall Cases

There are a number of advantages to renting a mall case or booth. Malls are usually well organized, clean, and have standard credit and discount policies. The mall personnel handle packing and wrapping for your customers, usually accept credit cards, and just charge you the service fee. Your presence may not be required, except to rotate stock, though some malls require dealers to put in a specified number of hours per month "tending the store."

On the other hand, it's easy for your merchandise to get lost in the crowd at a large mall with hundreds of showcases. And be sure to know the mall's policy on reproductions and fakes; if other dealers bring in junk, "quality" customers will stop coming. Also be sure you understand exactly what your costs are before signing an agreement. Some malls charge a percentage of your sales in addition to rent—an arrangement that may net you exactly zero. Malls tend to be susceptible to shoplifters, and the mall's insurance probably won't cover any losses you sustain.

Online Auctions

A great way to sell a few pieces or a whole collection, especially if you don't really want to become a dealer, is the online auction. You don't have to set up a shop or booth, you don't have to face the public, you don't even have to leave home!

You list items, along with photos, at an online auction. Potential customers will ask questions, you'll respond, and eventually you'll receive bids. You get paid before you ship the item, and the commission you pay the auction house is minimal.

There are a few minor drawbacks. You are dealing with someone you don't know, who may wear your jewelry and try to return it, or even switch it for another piece and try to get a refund. Merchandise can be damaged in shipping, and the buyer will certainly hold you responsible if it arrives broken or with a damaged stone. And there will be a small percentage of people who bid in your auction and then renege, leaving you to start over again.

Live Auctions

Auctions are a good way to sell a few important pieces or a large collection, but choose the auctioneer carefully. You want to find someone with considerable experience selling antique and collectible jewelry.

Find out where and how the auction house, or auctioneer, advertises. Ideally your items should be listed individually in the auctioneer's ads in order to attract an audience of serious bidders.

Specify how you wish your jewelry sold; otherwise, the auctioneer may simply make up groups of ten or a dozen unrelated items and sell them in lots, a method that will almost always reduce your profit.

Most auction houses have standard commission schedules, but they may be negotiable. If you're consigning a large collection to auction, you may be able to negotiate a better percentage.

Writing Accurate, Descriptive Ads

Laundry lists won't do, and you'll waste a lot of time, money, and effort with inadequate ads that won't attract anyone. Put yourself in the shoes of the reader and take the time to write a complete description for each jewel you want to sell.

Here's an example of an ad that gives enough information for a collector to know what it is you're selling (and to start drooling!):

Antique 14K gold brooch, approximately 1¾" high by 1½" wide. Its bezel surrounds an artist-signed ivory portrait cameo, c. 1875. The portrait is a left-facing woman in a draped gown with pearl necklace and intricately curled hair. The large, oval-shaped bezel is handmade for the one-of-a-kind cameo. Displays superb workmanship; the brooch is in excellent condition. Only $200—get it before it's gone.

Advertising

You may decide to sell by mail order, placing advertisements in trade papers yourself. Many people actually do make a living this way. It has the advantage of maintaining your privacy and—like the online dealer—you get paid before you ship merchandise. Caution: Think twice before including personal information, such as your home address or phone number, in a newspaper ad. Use a post office box or e-mail address.

The disadvantages are the costs of advertising and the limits of the papers' circulation. Be prepared for your sales to take quite a while and to run your ads repeatedly.

What's Sauce for the Goose . . .

Now that you've become the dealer (even temporarily, to sell your collection), there are a number of legal and ethical obligations:
1. You must collect—and pay—state sales taxes.
2. Income and profit (or loss) must be reported to the IRS.
3. Provide a written receipt for every sale. State all the terms and conditions of the sale, including your qualifications to make any guarantee as to authenticity.

Jewelry Parties

If you have a wide circle of friends and relatives who—in turn—have lots of friends, parties may be a fun and profitable way to market your jewelry.

The hostess gathers a group of people at her house for the purpose of viewing and buying jewelry. You set up, just as you would for a trade show, and it's a good idea to have a short informational presentation. It's a social event, and no one is under any obligation to buy, but they'll all tell their friends, and so on. Be sure to hand out plenty of business cards. And don't forget to give the hostess a nice piece of jewelry when the evening is over.

Donating a Collection

There are a number of good reasons for donating an important collection to an institution. You may want it to stay together in perpetuity, in the expert care of a curator. Perhaps your local museum or historical society is actively seeking permanent collections for the community. Or you'd simply rather have the tax deduction than sell your jewels.

The first step is to choose the museum, library, or other institution—make sure, of course, that it wants and is prepared to care for the collection. Work out the details in writing: how the jewelry is to be displayed, what credit you will receive, who is responsible for its proper care, whether it can ever be sold.

You will need to have the collection appraised if you want a tax deduction. The gift must go to a nonprofit organization with tax-exempt status. Check with an accountant to get proper guidance and conform to all the tax codes relevant to gifts of property.

And be sure you're ready to give it up. Once you donate it, it's gone.

References and Suggested Reading

The Official Identification and Price Guide to Antique Jewelry, 6th ed., by Arthur Guy Kaplan

Price Guide to Jewellery, 3,000 B.C. to 1950 A.D. by Michael Poynder

Warman's Jewelry, 2nd ed., by Christie Romero

Joseph Weisner rhinestone bracelet

Shows

Call or visit the promoters' Web sites for exact dates, which vary from year to year.

Atlantique City

Atlantic City, N.J.: March and October
Brimfield Promotions
(800) 526-2724
www.atlantiquecity.com

Bustamante Shows

Several specialized shows, including jewelry, in West Coast cities (Pasadena, San Francisco, Santa Clara, and Santa Monica)
P.O. Box 637
Atwater, CA 95301
(209) 358-3134
(209) 358-3756
www.bustamante-shows.com

Caskey & Lees
General and specialized shows in Los
Angeles, New York, Chicago, San
Francisco, and Santa Fe
P.O. Box 1409
Topanga, CA 90290
(310) 455-2886
www.artnet.com/artfairs/caskey2000.
asp

Farmington Antiques Weekend
Farmington, Conn.: June and September
Revival Promotions
(508) 839-9735
www.farmington-antiques.com

Triple Pier Expo
New York, N.Y.: November and March
Stella Show Management
(212) 255-0020
www.stellashows.com

**Vintage Clothing, Jewelry and
Textiles Show**
White Plains, NY: January
Stratford, Conn.: February
The Maven Co.
(914) 248-4646

Dealers Specializing in Jewelry

Our expert contributors have compiled this list of dedicated jewelry dealers, but neither they nor the publisher make any representations or guarantees pertaining to
your potential dealings with them. It's up to you to use the general information and
advice we've provided in this book to guide your specific purchasing.

Athena Antiques
100 Beta Drive
Franklin, TN 37064
(615) 377-3442
Antiques Unlimited Mall,
Murfreesboro, Tenn.; shows

Birch Hill Antiques
8010 Hickory Hill Lane
Huntsville, AL 35802
(205) 881-0483
Shows only

Echo's Past Antiques
322 Witthorne Drive
Cincinnati, OH 45226
(513) 821-9696
Shop

Harrice Miller Collection
Gallery #230
The Showplace
40 West 25th Street
New York, NY 10010
(212) 242-0910
harrice@worldnet.att.net

Just Jewelry
Kim Cummins
(618) 398-2173
www.jstjewelry.com

Liz Collectible Jewelry
Isabelle Bryman
P.O. Box 1368
Levittown, PA 19058
(215) 781-1174
ibryman@lizjewel.com
www.lizjewel.com

Morning Glory Antiques
Jane Clarke
Antique Connection Mall
12815 Central NE
Albuquerque, NM 87123
(505) 296-2300
www.morninggloryantiques.com

Mt. Washington Antiques
3742 Kellogg Avenue
Cincinnati, OH 45226
(513) 321-6584
Shop

Parure.com
www.parure.com
Owned by Pam Dini, a woman with
an eagle eye for the best in contemporary designer jewelry. Everything
is pristine. Contests with jewelry
giveaways and a wonderful picture
gallery where you can view the jewelry of many different sellers, up for
auction at various online venues.

RHUMBA!®
Terri Friedman
P.O. Box 148186
Chicago, IL 60614-8186
(773) 929-9007
www.tace.com/vendors/rhumba.htm
Friedman is an avid collector and
jewelry scholar. Her well-edited collection offers the best at every price
level. She sells antique to contemporary, all top quality and a good value.
She finds special things for you if
you let her know what you want.

Townline Antiques
2066 Brant Street, Unit 2
Burlington, Ontario, Canada
L7P3A6
(905) 335-5488
Two shops—St. Jacob Antique
Market and Jordan Antique Centres

**Valerie B. Gedziun Designer
Costume Jewelry**
www.valerieg.com
Gedziun carries nothing but the
best. She sells the top designers of
yesterday, today, and tomorrow; jewelry includes rare items in pristine
condition. Pricey, but you likely
won't see what you're wearing on
anyone else.

A Wink and a Smile
Judi Scheele
(972) 966-0092
www.winksmile.com

Auction Houses Dealing in Jewelry

Catalogs of completed as well as upcoming auctions featuring jewelry are available for sale from many of these auction houses. Call or write for catalog lists and auction schedules. Once you make contact, many auction houses will mail announcements to you on a regular basis.

Beverly Hills Auctioneers
9454 Wilshire Boulevard, Suite 202
Beverly Hills, CA 90212
(310) 278-8115/fax: (310) 278-5567

Butterfields
7601 Sunset Boulevard
Los Angeles, CA 90046
(323) 850-7500/fax: (323) 850-5843

Butterfields
220 San Bruno Avenue
San Francisco, CA 94103
(415) 861-7500/fax: (415) 861-8951

Christie's
Rockefeller Center
20 Rockefeller Plaza
New York, NY 10020
(212) 636-2000 fax: (212) 636-2399

Christie's East
219 East 67th Street
New York, NY 10021
(212) 606-0400/fax: (212) 452-2063

Christie's Los Angeles
360 North Camden Drive
Beverly Hills, CA 90210
(310) 385-2600/fax: (310) 385-9292

William Doyle Galleries
175 East 87th Street
New York, NY 10128
(212) 427-2730/fax: (212) 369-0892

Joseph DuMouchelle
199 North Main Street, Suite 204
Plymouth, MI 48170
(734) 455-4555/fax: (734) 455-2403

Native American Art Auctions
P.O. Box 705
Cloudcroft, NM 88317
(505) 687-3676/fax: (505) 687-3592

Rose Galleries
2717 Lincoln Drive
Roseville, MN 55113
(651) 484-1415
www.rosegalleries.com

C.G. Sloan and Company
4920 Wyaconda Road
Rockville, MD 20852
(301) 368-4911 or
(800) 649-5066
fax: (301) 468-9182

Sotheby's
1334 York Avenue
New York, NY 10021
(212) 606-7000/fax: (212) 606-7107

Sotheby's Beverly Hills
9665 Wilshire Boulevard
Beverly Hills, CA 90212
(310) 274-0340/fax: (310) 274-0899

Sotheby's Chicago
215 West Ohio Street
Chicago, IL 60610
(312) 396-9599/fax: (312) 396-9598

Treadway/Toomey Galleries
818 North Boulevard
Oak Park, IL 60301
(708) 383-5234/fax: (708) 383-4828

Weschler's
909 E Street NW
Washington, D.C. 20004
(202) 628-1281/fax: (202) 628-2366

Publications

Some of these publications are available only to members of collector's clubs and associations listed in the following section—usually included as a benefit for paying annual membership dues.

Antique Trader Weekly
P.O. Box 1050
Dubuque, IA 52001

Auction Forum USA
341 West 12th Street
New York, NY 10014

Glittering Times Newsletter
Editors/publishers: Davida
Baron/Terry Franzese
P.O. Box 656675
Fresh Meadows, NY
(718) 969-2320
E-mail:
glittering_times@bigfoot.com

Jewelers' Circular-Keystone
Cahners Business Publications
201 King of Prussia Road
Radnor, PA 19089-0140

The Loupe
Gemological Institute of America
World News
The Robert Mouawad Campus
5345 Armada Drive
Carlsbad, CA 92008

Modern Jeweler
P.O. Box 2939
Shawnee Mission, KS 66201

National Cufflink Society Newsletter
Editor: Eugene R. Klompus
P.O. Box 5700
Vernon, IL 60061
phone/fax: (847) 816-0035
www.cufflink.com

National Jeweler
1501 Broadway, Room 930
New York, NY 10036

Professional Jeweler
1500 Walnut Street, Suite 1201
Philadelphia, PA 19102
www.professionaljeweler.com

VFCJ
Newsletter for Vintage, Fashion, and
Costume Jewelry
Editor: Lucille Tempesta
P.O. Box 265
Glen Oaks, NY 11044
VFCJ@aol.com

Clubs and Collecting Associations

**The American Plastics History
Association**
534 Stublyn Road
Granville, OH 43023

**The American Society of Jewelry
Historians**
P.O. Box 103
1B Quaker Ridge Road
New Rochelle, NY 10804

Hairwork Society
P.O. Box 1617
Orem, UT 84059
www.hairwork.com

Jewelcollect
www.jewelcollect.org
Mail list server, member online message boards, annual charity costume jewelry auction

National Cufflink Society
P.O. Box 5700
Vernon, IL 60061
phone/fax: (847) 816-0035
www.cufflink.com

**Vintage, Fashion
and Costume Jewelry**
P.O. Box 265
Glen Oaks, NY 11044
Publishes quarterly newsletter by the same name. Biannual convention and sporadic mini-conventions.

Online Auctions

Amazon.com
www.amazon.com
Jewelry category or search by keyword: jewelry type (cameo, mosaic);
designer name (Weiss, Chanel); period (Victorian, Moderne); or material
(sterling, pearl).

eBay.com
www.eBay.com
Jewelry category listings:
http://pages.ebay.com/jewelry-
index.html
Keyword search: jewelry type
(cameo, mosaic); designer name
(Weiss, Chanel); period (Victorian,
Moderne); or material (sterling,
pearl).

Jewelcollect Auction
www.jewelcollect.org
An all-jewelry auction

Repair, Restoration, and Conservation Specialists

Antiques Restoration by Julian
Julian Pyatetsky
110 West 25th Street
New York, NY 10001
(212) 647-0305
Repairs and restores all jewelry,
makes duette mechanisms.

Javier Francisco Olivares
P.O. Box 35
Walnut Creek, CA 94596
(925) 937-7554
www.glitterbox.com/javi/repair.htm
Repairs Mexican and Scandinavian
sterling.

Jay Howard
14034 Ventura Boulevard
Sherman Oaks
Los Angeles, CA 91423
(818) 906-0807
Repairs and restores all costume
jewelry.

John Catalano
www.gate.net/~catalano
Repairs Eisenberg jewelry.

Sources of Reproduction Jewelry

Bernard Nacht & Co., Inc.
29 West 47th Street
New York, NY 10036
"Old World Styles"; catalog
available.

Fay Cullen
Suite 209
2124 N.E. 123 Street
North Miami, FL 33181
Art Nouveau–style gold enamel
flowers and Art Deco–style cufflinks

Heirloom 73
242 West 30th St.
New York, NY 10001
1920s-style filigree in gold, vermeil,
and sterling

Herzog and Adamms
37 West 47th St.
New York, NY 10036
Complete line of reproduction garnet
jewelry

Judith Jack, Inc.
27 West 47th St.
New York, NY 10036
Sterling marcasite Art Deco jewelry

Jewelry by Joshua
157 N.E. 166 Street
Miami Beach, FL 33163
Line of reproduction slides and slide
bracelets

K. Goldschmidt Jewelers, Inc.
25 West 47th Street
New York, NY 10036
Finely crafted 14K pieces with genuine stones

ANNOTATED BIBLIOGRAPHY

Jewelry History, Styles, and Techniques

Ball, Joanne Dubbs. *Costume Jewelers: The Golden Age of Design.* Schiffer Publishing, 1990. Organized by designer, this book has biographies and company histories of the best and brightest, with beautiful photos of their work.

Becker, Vivienne. *Antique and 20th Century Jewellery,* 2nd ed., NAG Press, 1989. Make this book a must for your library. It's a good guide for the collector and has great illustrations. Each chapter concentrates on a specific topic; it is easy to find information without having to read the entire book. Comprehensive cross-referencing among chapters.

_____. *Art Nouveau Jewelry.* Thames and Hudson, 1998. A fine introductory reference to an important movement in twentieth-century jewelry design.

Bell, C. Jeanenne. *Answers to Questions About Old Jewelry,* 1840–1950, 5th ed., Krause Publications, Inc., 1999. An excellent primer on Victorian and Edwardian jewelry, as well as jewelry of the first half of the twentieth century.

Burkholz, Matthew L. *The Bakelite Collection.* Schiffer, 1997. A beautiful book that visits collectors who got in on the ground floor and have stunning collections. You'll see things you never dreamed existed.

Cera, Deanna Farneti, ed. *Amazing Gems.* Harry N. Abrams, 1997. A gorgeous book, with lots of historical information as well.

———. *Jewels of Fantasy: Costume Jewelry of the 20th Century.* Harry N. Abrams, 1992. If you don't think costume jewelry is art, you will after you look at the photos in this book. Essays by some of the foremost authorities in the field.

Darling, Sharon S. *Chicago Metalsmiths.* Chicago Historical Society, 1977. Not everyone knows about this gem. Although its title and publisher might imply that the book is of only regional interest, don't be fooled. It has a lot of useful information.

Davis, Mary L., and Greta Pack. *Mexican Jewelry.* University of Texas Press, 1963. Although this book needs to be updated, it remains valuable for designer and marks information on still-popular Mexican jewelry.

Flower, Margaret. *Victorian Jewellery.* A. S. Barnes, 1951. Hard to find, but probably the most definitive book on Victorian jewelry, indispensable for the beginner and expert alike. Flower's work is the standard.

Goldemberg, Rose L. *Antique Jewelry: A Practical and Passionate Guide.* Crown Publishing, 1969. Don't let the title or the cover layout turn you off. This is a practical basic handbook. It discusses period jewelry available today—the pieces you're most likely to find. The book is invaluable whether you're starting a collection of jewelry or not.

Art Deco Fashion and Jewelry. Inc. Book Sales, 1998. Provides thoroughgoing background on all things Art Deco, relating jewelry to the fashion that inspired it.

Morrill, Penny C. and Carol A. Berk, *Mexican Silver: 20th Century Handwrought Jewelry and Metalwork.* Schiffer Publishing, 1994. An overview of the history of the silver industry in Taxco, with a primary focus on William Spratling, followed by additional chapters on other individual designers/silversmiths and workshops, including their marks.

Morrill, Penny C., *Silver Masters of Mexico.* Schiffer Publishing, 1996. Focuses on Héctor Aguilar, his workshop, and the people who worked for him, with some additional material on others, including marks.

Moro, Ginger. *European Designer Jewelry.* Schiffer Publishing, 1995. If you thought all costume jewelry was made in the United States, feast your eyes on this work of art. A weighty tome with gorgeous photos, arranged by country.

Sataloff, Joseph. *Art Nouveau Jewelry.* Dorrance & Company, 1984. More than a well-done practical guide to the history and beauty of Art Nouveau jewelry, Sataloff's book has a wonderful compendium of international jewelers' marks.

Tolkien, Tracy, and Henrietta Wilkinson. *A Collector's Guide to Costume Jewelry: Key Styles and How to Recognize Them.* Firefly Books, 1997. The subtitle is "key styles and how to recognize them," but this book provides more than that. It also has great historical information, color photography, and line drawings.

Untracht, Oppi. *Jewelry Concepts and Technology.* Doubleday, 1985. Covers every aspect of how jewelry is made, from historic to contemporary work. For a clear understanding—from A to Z—of what lies behind the jewelry-making mystique, this unique reference is for you.

von Neumann, Robert. *The Design and Creation of Jewelry,* 3rd ed., Chilton, 1982. A superb text on jewelry technique, from engraving, etching, and enameling to electroforming and reticulation. Covers basic lapidary and gem-cutting methods, as well as tools and supplies used for minor repairs.

Dictionaries

Mason, Anita, and Diane Packer. *An Illustrated Dictionary of Jewellery.* Harper & Row, 1978. An excellent addition to your library.

McNeil, Donald S. *Jewelers' Dictionary,* 3rd ed., Chilton, 1976. An American dictionary. Some terms can differ from the other two dictionaries listed here, which are British.

Newman, Harold. *An Illustrated Dictionary of Jewelry.* Thames and Hudson, 1994. A must for every library—period.

Marks

Banister, Judith, ed. *English Silver Hallmarks.* Foulsham & Co. Ltd., 1992. A handy, pocket-sized guide to carry with you.

JCK's Trade-Marks of the Jewelry and Kindred Trades. The Jewelers' Circular Publishing Co., 1972. This handy book has extensive illustrations of marks, registered and unregistered, used by manufacturers and dealers of jewelry, silverware, silver-plated ware, watches, watch cases, precious and imitation stones, clocks, fountain pens, tools, materials, cut glass, etc. Although badly out of date and difficult to find, it is the best available source.

Jewelers' Circular-Keystone Brand Name and Trademark Guide, 11th ed. Jewelers' Circular-Keystone, 1996. An identification guide to names and symbols used by makers of jewelry store products. Includes names and addresses of all companies listed. You can go to the JCK Web site at www.jckgroup.com to order their publications.

Paulson, Paul L. *Guide to Russian Silver Hallmarks.* Privately printed, 1976. Provides well-rounded coverage of Russian silver, including hallmarks, historical table, Cyrillic alphabet transliteration, important Russian silversmiths, assayers' marks, and other marks found on silver.

Rainwater, Dorothy T. *American Jewelry Manufacturers.* Schiffer Publishing, 1988. An alphabetically organized guide to makers' marks and names. A good companion to Ginger Moro's book on European designers, and an essential reference on American jewelry.

Tardy. *International Hallmarks on Silver.* Tardy, 1993. (21 Rue des Boulangers, 75505 Paris, France; 1-326-17-02). Originally published in French, this bible of international silver hallmarks was finally translated into English in 1981. It's a must for every library. Tardy's Les Poincons de Garantie Internationaux pour L'or, le Platine et le Palladium is the bible of international gold and platinum marks: keep your English/French dictionary close at hand.

Price Guides

Note: Many price guides contain historical and other useful information found nowhere else. If you use the prices, use them only as guidelines. No matter what the source, or how current prices are, they vary greatly by geographic region and are affected by condition, as well as supply and demand.

Baker, Lillian. *Art Nouveau and Art Deco Jewelry: An Identification and Value Guide.* Collector Books, 1997. This book presents "the diverse directions and paths that Art Nouveau and Art Deco periods stalked and shadowed." It has a concise table of contrasts, plus good illustrations throughout.

———. *Fifty Years of Collectible Jewelry.* Collector Books, 1995.

———. *One Hundred Years of Collectible Jewelry.* Collector Books, 1997. These two books cover not only old jewelry prices, but also jewelers' merchandise (e.g., hatpins, handbags). Baker's glossaries provide a wealth of easily understood information and conveniently include pronunciations.

Dolan, Maryanne. *Collecting Rhinestone and Colored Jewelry,* 4th ed., Krause Publications, Inc., 1998. The photos are in black and white (plus a color insert), but there's an extensive section on trademarks to help identify and date jewelry.

Kaplan, Arthur Guy. *The Official Identification and Price Guide to Antique Jewelry,* 6th ed., House of Collectibles, 1990. The best guide there is on the combination of the jewelry business and antique jewelry. It was carefully revised in each edition. The illustrations are fair, but the descriptions are good.

Lynnlee, J. L. *All that Glitters,* 3rd rev. ed., Schiffer Publishing, 1999. Among the newest guides to costume jewelry, an easy-to-read paperback with good illustrations, comments, and information on a variety of costume jewelry.

Miller, Harrice Simons. *Costume Jewelry Identification and Price Guide,* 2nd ed., Avon, 1994. Photos are black and white (plus a color insert), but there's so much background information here, you're sure to learn about the costume jewelers who interest you.

Poynder, Michael. *The Price Guide to Jewellery, 3,000 B.C.. to 1950 A.D.* Antique Collectors' Club, 1980. Illustrations and descriptions are terrific. Periodically, a price-revision list is available; it includes a synopsis of price trends in jewelry and pertinent investing tips. Note that pricing is applicable to the British market.

Romero, Christie. *Warman's Jewelry*, 2nd ed., Krause Publications, Inc., 1998. A good general reference. All photos are in black and white, except for a small center section, but this is a scholarly work.

Directories

Maloney, David. *Maloney's Antiques and Collectibles Resource Directory*, 5th ed. Antique Trader Books, 1999. Dealers, collectors, auctions, shows, repair and restoration experts, clubs, publications—anything and everything of conceivable interest to collectors is in this up-to-the-minute directory.

Materials Identification

Shatz, Sheryl G. *What's It Made Of?* 3rd ed., self-published, 1996. Ordering information: N6HC@aol.com.

GLOSSARY

aurora borealis: A multicolor-producing, light-reflecting coating on beads or surfaces of rhinestones.

baguette: A rectangular, narrow faceted stone.

Bakelite: Trade name used for any of various synthetic resins and plastics. When referring to jewelry, Bakelite means a phenolic resin, also called Catalin or Prystal (when translucent). It has a distinctive scent when rubbed, somewhat like formaldehyde.

baroque: A type of natural or cultured pearl with an uneven or craggy shape and surface.

base metal: Nonprecious alloys of copper, tin, lead, nickel, as well as alloys of these including other metals (zinc, antimony, etc.). Alloy "recipes" can vary in the percentages of the metals used. Commonly known alloys include brass, bronze, pinchbeck, pewter, white metal, nickel silver (German silver), and alpaca. "Pot metal" is a colloquial expression for white metal, which is an alloy of tin and lead.

bezel: Metal band used to hold stones in position.

bezel set: Set within a rim of metal.

brilliant cut: Circular gem with 58 facets. Also called *American cut* or *ideal cut.*

cabochon: A smooth-surfaced gemstone cut with no faceting.

C clasp: A simple closure, often called a *catch*, in the shape of a C, found on old brooches.

cameo: Stone, shell, or other material carved to leave a raised design above the table. The opposite of *intaglio.*

carat: Unit of weight for gemstones; 1 carat = 200 milligrams.

circa: (abbr. c. or ca.) Literally, "around" or "about," used to mean ten years before or after a given date. Never use circa when a piece of jewelry can be dated to an exact year.

cold painting: Applying paint to metal without firing it afterward.

crystal: Glass stone, bead, or other object with high lead content.

enamel: A glasslike mixture of silica, quartz, borax, feldspar, lead, and metallic oxides ground into fine powder, applied to an article (for jewelry, usually applied to metal) and fired.

faceting: The lapidary art of cutting a gemstone to produce many facets or planes.

faux: (abbr. f.) False, fake, imitation; e.g., *f. pearl* means imitation pearl.

findings: Small metal parts, such as clasps, used as components to make or repair jewelry. Findings are machine made, mass-produced.

fittings: Small metal components used in making or repairing jewelry. Fittings are handmade. See *findings.*

Florentine finish: A brushed or striated appearance on metal created by engraving

girdle: The edge of a brilliant-cut gem that is held by the setting.

gold: An element especially well suited to use in jewelry. It can be carved, cast, hammered, and alloyed with other metals. It is inert, so it will not oxidize or deteriorate. Purity is measured in karats; 24K is pure gold.

gold-filled: (abbr. g.f.) A form of plating over base metal, using lesser karat gold, such as 10K, usually 1/20K or 1/12K.

gold tone: Gold in color.

gold wash: A thin coat of gold, usually electroplated, not measurable in karats.

hairwork: Braided or designed hair made into jewelry.

intaglio: Recessed design carved into the surface of a stone. Opposite of *cameo.*

jet: A stone made of petrified coal. *French jet* is a term used for black glass.

karat: Unit of fineness for gold; 1 karat is equal to 1/24 part pure gold in an alloy.

Lucite®: Acrylic thermoplastic; DuPont registered trade name.

marcasite: Iron pyrite. A faceted stone often used in jewelry, sometimes confused with pyrite or fool's gold.

marquise: A faceted oval or elliptical stone, pointed at both ends (also called *navette*).

marriage, married jewelry: Jewelry made by combining parts of two or more different pieces of jewelry.

mourning jewelry: Created and worn in remembrance of dead friends or relatives. May have hair compartment. When enameled, the color used is black or blue. See also *hairwork.*

old European cut: Faceted gem with a circular shape and large culet (the bottom facet parallel to the table). Table diameter is usually 50% or less than that of the girdle.

old mine cut: Gem faceted with a cushion shape. The girdle is placed halfway between the top and bottom of the stone for a squarish appearance.

parure: A complete set of jewelry, made to match. A full parure should consist of a necklace, brooch, bracelet, and earrings. A three-piece set is a *demi-parure.* Two pieces are a set.

pâte de verre: Literally, "glass paste." A type of molded colored glass.

pavé: Small stones set closely together on a metal surface.

pot metal: See *base metal.*

pronged: Stones set with individual prongs to hold them in place.

rhinestone: A glass stone, clear or colored, faceted to imitate a precious gemstone, such as diamond or ruby. Compare to *synthetic gemstones.*

rose cut: A method of cutting stones with a circular or squarish flat base, rising to a faceted pointed top.

safety catch or clasp: Closure for brooches with an added mechanism to prevent accidental opening.

seed pearl: A tiny imitation pearl, or faux pearl.

silver tone: Silver in color—may not be silver at all.

stamped: Made by die-stamping a sheet of metal; durable if in thick metal or sterling silver, not so durable if in brass or thin metal.

sterling silver: 925 parts silver (to 75 parts copper) is the legal standard. In comparison, coin silver is 900 parts, Continental silver is 800.

synthetic gemstones: Laboratory-created stones that are identical chemically, optically, and physically to the natural gemstones. Most synthetic gemstones are called by their equivalent natural names prefaced by the word "synthetic," e.g. synthetic ruby. Igmerald is a trade name for the man-made equivalent of emerald. Another is Chatham-created emeralds. Cubic zirconia, by exception, is a diamond simulant, not a true synthetic diamond. Synthetic gemstones should not be confused with imitation stones, which are only similar in appearance, not in physical properties, to gemstones.

table: the uppermost flat surface of a cut gem.

ABOUT THE INTERNATIONAL SOCIETY OF APPRAISERS

The Collector's Compass series is endorsed by the International Society of Appraisers, one of North America's leading nonprofit associations of professionally educated and certified personal property appraisers. Members of the ISA include many of the industry's most respected independent appraisers, auctioneers, and dealers. ISA appraisers specialize in over 200 areas of expertise in four main specialty pathways: antiques and residential contents, fine art, gems and jewelry, and machinery and equipment.

Established in 1979 and consisting of over 1,375 members, the ISA is founded on two core principles: educating its members through a wide range of continuing education and training opportunities, and promoting and maintaining the highest ethical and professional standards in the field of appraisals.

Education through the ISA

In conjunction with the University of Maryland University College, the ISA offers a series of post-secondary professional courses in appraisal studies, including a two-level certification program.

The ISA recognizes three membership levels within its organization—Associate Member, Accredited Member, and Certified Member—with educational programs in place for achieving higher distinctions within the society. ISA members who complete the required coursework are recognized with the title of Certified Appraiser of Personal Property (CAPP). Through its pioneering education programs, the ISA plays a vital role in producing qualified appraisers educated in appraisal theory, principles, procedures, ethics, and law as it pertains to personal property appraisal.

Professional Standards of the ISA

The ISA is dedicated to the highest ethical standards of conduct, ensuring public confidence in the ability and qualifications of its members. To help members perform their work with the most up-to-date knowledge of professional standards, the ISA is continually updating, expanding, and improving its courses and criteria of conduct.

For more information about the International Society of Appraisers, contact their corporate offices at:

Toll-free: 1-800-472-4732
E-mail: ISAHQ@isa-appraisers.org
Web:www.isa-appraisers.org

ABOUT THE CONTRIBUTORS

Judith Katz-Schwartz was born and raised in New York City. She began running a part-time antiques and collectibles business while still working as an executive chef and corporate food executive. It wasn't long before she took the full-time plunge, founding Twin Brooks Antiques and Collectibles in 1986. In 1987 she opened a professional independent appraisal practice. Since 1993, Ms. Katz-Schwartz has also been doing business online, via her Twin Brooks Web site (www.msjudith.net).

Numerous television programs have featured Ms. Katz-Schwartz as a collectibles expert, and she currently appears on the Pax-TV Network show *Treasures in Your Home.* Her enormous collection of vintage costume jewelry has become her signature wherevr she goes.

Ms. Katz-Schwartz writes, edits, and publishes the *Antiques and Collectibles Newsletter,* an offbeat weekly e-mail newsletter about collecting. She writes for *Antiqueweek, Thompsons' Antiques Gazette,* and *Unravel the Gavel* as well as Auction Universe and Prodigy's online collectibles newsletter, and gives frequent seminars on antiques and collectibles around the United States. She is a member of the International Society of Appraisers and the Association of Online Appraisers.

A collector of more things than she cares to ponder, Judith Katz-Schwartz lives in Manhattan and Sullivan County, New York, with her husband, Arthur Schwartz.

Elaine J. Laurtes, G.G., a graduate of the Gemological Institute of America, became interested in old jewelry around 1970 when she avidly began collecting, then selling, antiques. She is a Charter Member of the International Society of Appraisers, served on their Board of Directors, and was the Chairman of the Appraisal Services Committee. In 1985 she was presented the ISA Distinguished Service Award, and in 1987 the Certificate of Appreciation Award. Mrs. Luartes has published articles and lectured on various topics in old jewelry, most recently at Kent State University.

In the past, Mrs. Luartes has served as Regional Director for the National Association of Dealers in Antiques, President of the Minnesota Antiques Dealers Association, and held membership in ISA, NADA, Accredited Gemologists Association, Association of Women Gemologists, and the Society of Jewelry Historians— USA.

Elaine Luartes and her husband, Bob, are semiretired, own Athena Antiques, and reside near Nashville, Tennessee.

Christopher J. Kuppig has spent his entire career in book publishing. For several years he directed programs at Dell Publishing, Consumer Reports Books, and most recently Chilton Book Company—where his assignment included managing the Wallace-Homestead and Warman's lines of antiques and collectibles guides.

In 1997, Mr. Kuppig founded Stone Studio Publishing Services, a general management consultancy to book publishers. Acting as Series Editor for the Collector's Compass has given him the opportunity to draw upon his wide-ranging network of contacts in the collecting field.

Mr. Kuppig resides with his wife and three children in eastern Massachusetts.